Teams
at the TOP

Unleashing the Potential of *Both* Teams and Individual Leaders

JON R. KATZENBACH

Harvard Business School Press
Boston, Massachusetts

Printed in the United States of America

01 00 99 98 97   5 4 3 2 1

Library of Congress Cataloging-in-Publication Data

Katzenbach, Jon R., 1932–
   Teams at the top : unleashing the potential of both teams and individual leaders /
Jon R. Katzenbach.
      p.   cm.
   Includes bibliographical references and index.
   ISBN 0-87584-789-7
   1. Teams in the workplace.   2. Leadership.   I. Title.
HD66.K383   1997
658.4'02—dc21   97-26322
                                                                         CIP

The paper used in this publication meets the requirements of the American National
Standard for Permanence of Paper for Printed Library Materials Z39.49-1984

To my wife, Linda, whose faith in me never wavers.

Contents

Acknowledgments

Of the many people who helped with this book, my first acknowledgments go to those senior executives who shared their experiences— positive and negative—with me. Some were clients, of course, but most were not. Only two asked not to be identified in the book, and three were more comfortable in disguised examples. Dozens of others, however, were most generous in allowing me to learn about, comment on, and interpret their experiences—even when it cast them in a less than favorable light. I truly appreciate their openness, insight, and cooperation, without which the book would be much less realistic.

Next, I would like to thank a small group who helped me nourish the initial idea, and enabled me to develop it. Of my partners and colleagues, William Matassoni was the first to suggest the topic to me, and Roger Kline, Larry Kanarek, and Steven Dichter saw the potential in my early drafts. Richard Cavanagh, executive director of The Conference Board, as he has so many times before, provided sage counsel and insights on the substance of the material.

The real work, however, was shouldered mostly by my assistants, Debbie Shortnacy and Lisa Rawlings. Lisa, in particular, managed a vast array of case write-ups, drafts, redrafts, and revisions. She somehow tracked us through more than ten complete versions before a final manuscript emerged. In addition, Gene Zelazny deserves special thanks for his creative contributions to the charts, tables, and exhibits. Of course, the professionals at Harvard Business School Press were diligent throughout, and I particularly appreciate the wise counsel and advice of Marjorie Williams in helping shape and clarify my arguments and messages—and in urging me to take the time to get it right.

Most importantly, however, I wish to acknowledge the invaluable and special contributions of Nancy Taubenslag and Linda Katzenbach. Nancy, as she did for *Wisdom of Teams*, led the research and worked with me to develop the cases, verify the facts, question the logic, and suggest substantive content improvement. My wife, Linda, was far and away my most diligent, thoughtful, and insightful reader and editor. She read each and every draft, questioned each and every hypothesis, and edited all materials for both substance and grammatical correctness. Most importantly, she made me defend every assertion and conclusion. Much of the credit for the clarity, readability, continuity, and conciseness of the material belongs to her.

The Spirit of Haida Gwaii, sculpted by Bill Reid, is located outside the Canadian Embassy in Washington, D.C.

Introduction—
The Spirit of Haida Gwaii

ONE OF THE MORE WIDELY ACCLAIMED North American sculptures of the twentieth century rests in a reflecting pool at the Canadian Embassy in Washington, D.C. John W. Creighton, Jr., CEO of Weyerhaeuser, first called it to my attention a few days after a talk we had about his emerging "team at the top"—and the challenge he saw in getting all of them "into the same boat" with him. The sculpture, with its 13 grim-faced creatures cast in bronze, all crowded together in an ancient Haida canoe, all rowing to the apparent cadence of their leader, brings to mind a classic team at the top.

Of course, its creator never intended *The Spirit of Haida Gwaii* to be emblematic of teams at the top. Sculptor Bill Reid, a native Haida Indian from British Columbia, has drawn his inspiration from a living web of stories drawn out of the rich and complex mythology of the ancient Haida culture. Clearly, that legend and Reid's sculpture embody a much nobler purpose than any team could envision.

> The canoe contains both Raven and Eagle, women and men, a rich man and a poorer man, and animals as well as human beings. Is it fair, then to see in it an image not only of one culture but of the entire family of living things? There are nervous faces and tempers running high. But whatever their differences, they are paddling together, in one boat, headed in one direction. Wherever their journey takes them, let us wish them luck.[1]

Nonetheless, the sculpture captures for me the essence of why we seldom see teams at the top achieve real team levels of performance.

They may row to the cadence of a single leader, but they each have their hands full just holding onto their own oars. I presumed that, other than making joint decisions and reviewing the work of others, they could do little productive, hands-on work as a group, nor could they shift the leadership mantle among members as real teams do. I believed that the doctrine of individual accountability was simply too strong at the executive level to accommodate real teams. It also seemed to me that demands on top executives' time, due to their pursuit of important individual leadership activities, were too great to allow time for the "storming and forming" that help develop common levels of commitment in real teams. Top executives are expected to align the actions of large numbers of people—not to work within the confines of small groups or teams.

These early presumptions on my part, although perhaps understandable, were largely mistaken. In addition, the reality of senior leadership groups and team efforts has been changing rapidly. There are now more and more executives who recognize and pursue the potential for real team performance at the top, largely because the increasing pace of change demands greater leadership capacity than ever before—and, make no mistake, real teams do increase leadership capacity at any level. Additionally, the relentless search for growth and performance reaches outside and beyond whatever disaggregations of business units may exist. To ignore in this search the potential of team performance—in both the formal and the social contexts of organizations—would be shortsighted.

There is little question that such forces are producing a need for more rigorous and discriminating application of team performance discipline at the top than ever before. This does not, however, imply that *all* of a CEO's direct reports should become an ongoing "real team" or even function periodically as a real team. It does imply that senior leaders should know when the disciplined set of behaviors required for real team performance* should take priority over the equally disciplined—but different—behavior required for individual executive leadership performance, and vice versa.

---

*As defined later in this book and in Jon R. Katzenbach and Douglas K. Smith, *The Wisdom of Teams* (Boston: Harvard Business School Press, 1993).

WHAT THIS BOOK IS ABOUT

This book's central thesis is that *an integrated balance of real team, individual, and single-leader working group performance is both possible and desirable at the top*—not that one mode of behavior is intrinsically better than the other. Consequently, some readers may be confused, perhaps disappointed, to find that this book does not attempt to either prove or disprove that companies run by real teams at the top yield higher returns for shareholders or better value for customers. Neither the evidence obtained nor the examples selected provide such proof, nor is it a central argument of this book. In fact, most of the available or observable evidence actually points the other way. For example,

■ The best-performing companies are run by strong CEOs who function in single-leader working group configurations rather than in teams.

■ Self-proclaimed "teams at the top" typically fail to deliver acceptable returns to shareholders or customers.

■ Most observers of senior leadership groups do not recognize where, why, or how they perform as real teams.

This book is intended primarily for those who already believe, as a result of their own experiences, that real team behaviors *in the right places* can improve overall performance. Consequently, I have drawn on a range of successful and unsuccessful top team efforts and examples to argue that senior leadership groups have the opportunity to obtain a better balance between real team and single-leader capabilities. It stands to reason that getting the right balance between the two will both optimize performance capability and increase leadership capacity at the top. Those who already believe, as I do, that a real team can and does outperform a single-leader unit, when deployed against a legitimate team opportunity, should find this thesis of interest. Those who seek additional evidence that an ongoing "team at the top"* is somehow better or worse than a "nonteam" will not find it here.

---

*This term is set off with quotation marks to emphasize that a team at the top is rarely a team as defined in *The Wisdom of Teams*.

"TEAM AT THE TOP" IS A SEDUCTIVE NOTION

Virtually every thoughtful chief executive seeks his own "team at the top." The notion is probably as old as most human, if not animal, social orders. The term implies a strong, cohesive, complementary group of people who pull together in support of the leader's vision and aspirations. Typically, however, they observe a clear "pecking order" that precludes real team performance. History is replete with examples of leaders who went to great lengths to ensure the kind of loyalty, dedication, and support implicit in the top team notion, using everything from coercion to inspiration to attain those ends. Pharaohs, kings, dictators, and presidents have always sought a tight, loyal "team at the top" on which they could rely against all opposition. Of course, they did not always use that label, nor did they often obtain that kind of result.

A team at the top is a seductive notion. Thus new CEOs reshape their own version of a top team to fit their image of what kind of support they will need from their leadership group. The business press perpetuates the view that CEOs of large organizations put together a top team of executives to spearhead their enterprise. But we all know that these so-called top teams seldom function as real teams because of the pressures of other priorities, as well as their strong desire to preserve individual accountability, if not ego. They neither shift the leadership role nor apply the basic discipline required for real team performance results. In *The Wisdom of Teams*, Douglas Smith and I defined that discipline as

> a *small number* of people with *complementary skills* who are committed to a *common purpose, performance goals, and approach* for which they hold themselves *mutually accountable*.[2]

Each phrase highlighted in italics represents an explicit element of discipline—what we called "team basics"—that is absolutely essential if a working group (at any level) is to obtain the extra measure of performance results that real teams can deliver.

Walk into almost any organization of any size in any sector of the economy and ask anyone below the top about the "team at the top." Their immediate response is a knowing smile of skepticism, followed by a comment that implies "Well, they're not really a team, but. . . ." Even in the best of companies—particularly if you happen to talk to someone who has been a member of a real team down the line—it is well accepted that the term *top team* rarely means "real team." The CEO invariably functions as the single leader of a group whose membership is based on formal positions rather than on individual skills, whose purpose and goals are indistinguishable from the overall corporate purpose and goals, and whose behaviors are determined entirely by individual accountability. Hence, although the group may proudly wear the team label, it does not function as a real team, nor does it achieve its potential performance as a leadership group. Simply put, it does not apply the "team basics."

By now it is perhaps obvious that the prevailing mindset makes an either/or assumption about team behaviors and precludes an effective integration with valid executive leadership behaviors. I believe it is important and possible to change both the mindset and its accompanying assumptions—to the ultimate benefit of a better-balanced leadership approach at the top.

A DIFFERENT MINDSET

"Team at the top" is a misused term that obscures both the practical options and the critical disciplines that top leaders can employ. All of the CEO's direct reports can seldom, if ever, constitute an ongoing real team. Nor should they try to become one in their quest for the high-performing enterprise. It simply does not work that way at the top, largely because of conflicting executive priorities, changing marketplace demands, individual accountability disciplines, and prevailing stakeholder expectations. Nonetheless, *high-performing organizations increasingly require a flexible and balanced leadership effort that fully exploits nonteam as well as team approaches.*

When we think of a team at the top made up only of the CEO's direct reports, we presume that all companies have one, for better or for worse. We also presume that this senior group of executives can function together only in one of two fundamental ways: as a hierarchical group or as a collaborative team. If those are the options, then most top teams certainly are not real teams, because the CEO calls the shots. Moreover, it is virtually impossible to change that pattern without changing the style of the CEO, which hardly ever happens. Hence, we observe very little team performance at the top of most companies.

To understand this book's line of argument, the reader should adopt a different mindset from the beginning. Picture a flexible group that functions in different modes of group behavior and composition— rather than "all of the CEO's direct reports," who must either function as a real team or not. The latter all-or-nothing viewpoint leads to two different kinds of myths about so-called teams at the top: strong leader myths and real team myths.

Strong Leader Myths

Those who favor strong executive leadership assume that strong top leaders cannot—and probably need not—function as a real team; that sort of behavior makes more sense down the line or in the workplace. This premise leads to five constraints or myths that are actually contrary to the reality of senior leadership behavior patterns.

1. *The CEO determines whether a company wins or loses.* What board of directors does not believe that, if you pick the right CEO, your problems will be solved? This view is held even more widely than by boards of directors, however; analysts, consultants, and journalists, as well as most executives, appear to agree. In fact, it is close to heresy for someone like me to suggest otherwise.

   The reality is that the leadership requirements of winning companies (particularly those that stand the test of time) go well beyond the CEO. It is not that the CEO role is somehow less important, or that the CEO's personal attributes have little influence on corporate performance; obviously, they do. Rather, it is the broad leadership and organizational systems that are more important over time. The research effort that led to *Built to Last* provides convincing evidence for the authors' statement about the top leaders in their "visionary companies":

   > . . . we're asking you to see the success of visionary companies—at least in part—as coming from underlying processes and fundamental dynamics embedded in the organization and not primarily the result of a single great idea or some great,

all-knowing, godlike visionary who made great decisions, had great charisma, and led with great authority.[3]

2. ***The CEO has to be in charge at all times.*** This myth says that, unless the CEO takes direct responsibility for making the key decisions, he or she cannot expect to have a high-performing company. No self-respecting top leader admits to backing off when a tough decision is needed. This is particularly true in turnaround situations. This view causes most of us to believe that a real team (wherein the leadership role shifts among the members) is really impossible at the top, because real teams do not limit themselves to a single leader or decision maker.

The reality is that the CEOs of large companies cannot make all the key decisions, nor do they try. Instead, a strong cadre of leaders down the line are making key decisions all the time that never reach the attention of the CEO. More and more companies are disaggregating their businesses to develop more decision makers closer to both the marketplace and the workplace. A further, highly relevant reality is that real teams can and do function within a construct at the top that permits the chief executive to decide key issues. But this need not prevent a shifting of leadership roles within team opportunities that require it.

3. ***It's a team because they say so!*** Leading executives, analysts, consultants, academics, and writers freely label the senior leadership groups of large and small companies "the team at the top." Moreover, there are very few CEOs who do not refer often, both privately and publicly, to their "top team." Everyone knows who they mean, despite the nonteam behavior that generally characterizes these groups.

The reality, which everyone knows as well, is that these groups seldom, if ever, function as a "real team" if one is rigorous about defining the term, applying the discipline it implies, and measuring the kind of results it should produce. Labeling the leadership group a "team" does not make it so.

4. ***The right person in the right job naturally leads to the right team.*** This myth assumes that teams will happen naturally if the right people are held individually responsible. The very best compa-

nies devote major portions of their human resource system to getting right person–right job match-ups. At some companies this becomes a slogan, if not a performance theme. At the top, the primary focus of new leaders is how to structure and fill the top jobs in the company—particularly those that comprise the CEO's direct reports. The understandable presumption is that the right person will somehow figure out how to shape his or her own top team and will instinctively team up with other executives as needed to get the job done.

The reality is that real teams at the top happen naturally only when a major unexpected event forces the issue—and only when the instincts of the senior leader permit the discipline of team performance to be applied. Unfortunately, that means that a great many valid team opportunities are being overlooked at the top of most companies.

5. *The top team's purpose is the corporate mission.* This myth assumes that the purpose of the top leadership group is to carry out the mission and strategy of the company. Although this is true, it seldom provides the kind of focus on collective work products or joint leadership that is required to produce common levels of commitment across the team.

The reality is that achievement of the company mission requires much more than what a small group of top leaders decides or does. Hence, it will not provide the focus, commitment, and mutual accountability that a real team effort must have. Although it is possible for senior leadership groups to shape more appropriate team performance purposes, they seldom do.

As understandable as the above myths may be, the result of holding onto any or all of them is to virtually preclude real team performance at the top—except where random events break the strong executive leadership discipline that prevails.

Real Team Myths

Equally constraining is a set of strongly held beliefs about the importance and potential value of real team performance within a senior leadership group. These beliefs are increasingly evident among top executives and have been at the heart of much of the research that has been published about team behaviors at the top. Unfortunately, they are as limiting and counterproductive as the strong leader myths just described. Five in particular hamper the very team performance they are designed to stimulate:

1. ***Teamwork at the top will lead to team performance.*** This myth argues for more attention to the "four Cs" of effective teamwork: communication, cooperation, collaboration, and compromise. It also recognizes that senior leadership groups need to practice more supportive behaviors or teamwork. In fact, most of us assume that this is probably the only kind of team effort that senior groups can be expected to pursue.

    The reality is that teamwork is not the same thing as team performance. Teamwork is broad-based cooperation and supportive behavior; a team is a tightly focused performance unit. By focusing all of their attention on teamwork, the senior group is actually less likely to be discriminating about when and where it needs to apply the discipline required to achieve real team performance. The group may improve its ability to communicate and support one another, but it will not obtain team performance without applying the explicit discipline required.

2. ***Top teams need to spend more time together building consensus.*** This myth presumes that time together will lead to team performance. It assumes that consensus decisions are invariably better than individual decisions, particularly with respect to the more critical corporate decisions and actions. Unfortunately, it also assumes that building consensus is synonymous with reducing conflict and that less conflict somehow leads to more teamlike behavior.

    The reality is that most executives have little time to spare as it is, and the idea of consuming more of that scarce resource struggling to build consensus makes little or no sense to them. In fact, a great many decisions are better made individually than collectively. Moreover, spending time together seeking consensus is not the same thing as doing real work together that yields a higher-performance result within a real team construct. The further reality here is that, in a real team, the right person or persons make the decisions; group consensus is not required. Most importantly, real team efforts do not avoid conflict; *they thrive on it,* and it is virtually unavoidable at the top. In fact, "top management teams typically face situations with high ambiguity, high stakes, and extreme uncertainty. Discord, contention, debate, disagreement—in short, conflict—are natural in such situations."[4]

3. *CEOs must change their personal style to obtain team perform-ance.* This myth says that the strong, decisive style of the CEO and other executives is the major culprit with respect to their lack of team performance. Followers of this myth frequently admonish top executives to abandon the basic discipline of executive leader-ship, back off from making all key decisions, and learn to be more teamlike in their behaviors. Some even advocate personal counsel-ing and leadership training to that end.

   The reality is that most top executives cannot materially change their style. Moreover, if they simply learn to play different roles instead, they can often behave in ways that stimulate real team efforts, if not function as members and leaders of such efforts. The basic beliefs, attitudes, and roles of senior leaders turn out to be much more important than their intrinsic leadership styles.

4. *The senior group should function as a team whenever it is to-gether.* This myth suggests that every task for the senior leadership group qualifies as a team opportunity, regardless of how that task is best carried out within the group. This leads to team-building sessions that can drive tough, skeptical executives up the wall. As a result, a lot of time can be wasted attempting to achieve team behaviors in situations that warrant more efficient, leader-driven approaches.

   The reality is that most senior leadership interactions are not real team opportunities and do not warrant the application of team discipline. Team efforts at the top make sense only part of the time. Nonteam efforts can often be faster and more effective, particularly when the value of the collective work products are either difficult to identify or not compelling.

5. *Teams at the top need to "set the example."* This myth presumes that teams down the line cannot be expected to perform as real teams unless the top leaders set an example in their actions to-

gether. The more avid believers in this view often argue for "daily examples" among the group.

The reality is that daily contact is seldom even possible among the members. Fortunately, most real team efforts down the line are unaffected by how the senior leadership group behaves, as long as the top leaders believe in the value of team performance down the line and are supportive of such team efforts. The support matters far more than the example. Moreover, many team efforts at the top are of necessity carried out "behind closed doors" because of the confidential nature of the crisis events that produce such behaviors.

As with myths growing out of the strong leader premise, those that grow out of the real team premise can be equally constraining on senior leadership performance as a group (Table I.1 summarizes these myths and realities). For that reason, this book both presumes and requires a different mindset, which seeks to integrate these two extreme points of view. Simply stated, a "team at the top" should be able to *vary its composition, behavior pattern, and leadership approach to optimize and better integrate individual, team, and nonteam performance.*

THREE MAJOR MESSAGES

A fundamental premise of this book is that the pursuit of *more undisciplined team efforts at the top usually inhibits—and therefore actually leads to fewer—real team levels of performance.* Within that context, this book focuses on three basic messages:

1. The best senior leadership groups are rarely a true team at the top—although they can and do function as real teams when major, unexpected events prompt that behavior.
2. Most of them can optimize their performance as a group by consciously working to obtain a better balance between their team and nonteam efforts—rather than by trying to become an ongoing single team.
3. The secret to a better balance lies in learning to integrate the discipline required for team performance with the discipline of executive (single-leader) behavior—not in replacing one with the other.

It is tempting for the proponents of individual leadership to believe that a strong chief executive, supported by a cadre of able and disci-

Table I.1

MYTHS AND REALITIES OF TEAMS AT THE TOP

Strong Leader Myths	The Realities
1. The CEO determines whether a company wins or loses.	1. Broad leadership and organizational systems are more important over time.
2. The CEO has to be in charge at all times.	2. CEOs of large companies cannot make all the key decisions; a strong cadre of leaders down the line makes key decisions as well.
3. It is a team because they say so!	3. The CEO's direct reports seldom, if ever, function as a real team on an ongoing basis.
4. The right person in the right job naturally leads to the right team.	4. "Right person, right job" is only part of a separate discipline required to achieve real team levels of performance.
5. The top team's purpose is the corporate mission.	5. Overall mission and strategy cannot form the purpose or goals for a real team; they lack the focus, commitment, and mutual accountability for team results.

Real Team Myths	The Realities
1. Teamwork at the top will lead to team performance.	1. Teamwork is not the same thing as team performance and often obscures real team performance opportunities.
2. Top teams need to spend more time together building consensus.	2. Leaders have no time to spare, and many decisions are best made individually; real teams do not seek consensus or conflict reduction.
3. CEOs must change their personal style to obtain team performance.	3. Team performance depends on CEO attitudes, beliefs, and roles—not on personal style.
4. The senior group should function as a team whenever it is together.	4. Most senior leadership interactions are not real team opportunities and do not warrant the application of team discipline.

Table I.1 *(continued)*
Myths and Realities of Teams at the Top

Real Team Myths	The Realities
5. Teams at the top need to "set the example."	5. Most real teams down the line are unaffected by how the senior leadership group behaves—as long as it is supportive of teams below.

plined top executives in solidly defined, formal leadership roles, can sustain a high-performing organization. Obviously, there is more to sustaining high performance over time than a set of strong executives performing well in critical top jobs.

It is also tempting for proponents of teams to believe that a strong team at the top is a more powerful way to lead a high-performance organization. Seldom is this the case either. The fact is that it is difficult, if not impossible, to identify a high-performance organization that has stood the test of time *because* it was led by a real team. That is not how high-performance organizations benefit from real team performance.

All too often, the "personal favorite" approaches of top leaders fall short, because they overrely on (and therefore misapply) them. In almost every sector of our economy we see upstarts like Compaq and Microsoft displacing IBM, or Home Depot displacing Kmart. And we see top leaders changed and changed again by nervous boards, who see no other recourse. The pace of change, the intensity of competition, the power of technology, and the unpredictability of our economic and social environments make adherence to any single leadership approach suspect—particularly if that approach is inflexible relative to both marketplace and workplace change. As a result, the best leaders are constantly reshaping their leadership composition and approach. Most appropriately, they are never satisfied.

Few well-managed companies today debate the value of increasing their overall leadership capacity. Most top leaders see a significant performance potential in building their leadership capacity at the top and are continually probing for ways to accomplish that. Such groups can and should learn to shift into—and out of—a team mode more consciously and rigorously than they do—but not necessarily more often. This will enable them to tap their full performance potential as a group. *The secret, however, is not to replace single-leader modes of behavior at the top with teams, but rather to integrate the two.* Unfortunately, this is not the understanding that most people have when referring to a "team at the top."

Terminology becomes important here. As we are undisciplined in our language, we become undisciplined in our thinking and actions. An undisciplined leadership group can suffer in its performance on both team and nonteam dimensions simply by pursuing "more team efforts" instead of "more real team levels of performance." The difference is significant. The terminology and definitions used in this book to describe senior leadership situations are critical to both understanding and applying the lessons of these situations. For that reason, Appendix A at the end of the book contains a glossary of "team terms," which defines some of the more important words and phrases used throughout the book, and Appendix B elaborates on the particular terminology used in team discipline. These appendices define terms that can have a meaning different in common usage from the explicit meaning used in this book.

WHAT IS DIFFERENT ABOUT THIS BOOK

The fundamental difference between this book and other excellent writings on the topic of top teams stems from its purpose, which is to convince the reader that *discipline is more important than teams at the top.* In other words, applying the right discipline in the right places at the right times is more important than trying to become a single real team at the top. There is considerable academic research and writing on the subject of top teams and leadership groups. Much of it, though excellent when judged against the common purpose of understanding how top groups can work together better, presumes a different definition of *team.* For example, Donald Hambrick defines it as follows: "a top management group qualifies as a team to the extent it engages in mutual and collective interaction. More tangibly, this is gauged by quantity and quality of information exchange, collaborative behavior and joint decision making."[5]

Certainly this is a useful definition for Hambrick's purposes. He and Sydney Finkelstein, in their book *Strategic Leadership: Top Executives and Their Effects on Organizations*,[6] also provide an excellent compendium and commentary on the academic literature about top management teams as defined above.

This book, however, takes a different tack. It postulates a higher hurdle (or at least a different standard) for judging team efforts at the top. While clearly encompassing the notions of mutual and collective interaction in Hambrick's definition, it also emphasizes what I will call the three litmus tests of a true performance team (or real team) at any level:

1. Mutual accountability for group results
2. Collective or joint work products of clear performance value
3. A sharing and/or shifting of leadership role among the members

These are tough tests to pass, particularly within a top leadership group. As a result, this book explores when, why, and how senior leadership groups can and do function to meet those tests and obtain real team performance. Most importantly, perhaps, it describes how to determine when nonteam efforts should prevail, and how to integrate both of these two very different disciplines (team and individual executive or nonteam) into a better-balanced top leadership approach. This book presumes that both approaches have value at the top of organizations that seek to increase the performance and leadership capacity of their senior executive groups.

THE LINE OF ARGUMENT BY CHAPTER

This book elaborates on why and how this hidden potential in achieving a better-balanced top leadership approach can be tapped and applied to obtain significant performance gains throughout any organization, large or small. The book's line of argument can be summarized as follows:

▪ Real team efforts at the top are in direct conflict with the strong single-leader approaches that exist in organizations of different cultures; it is very difficult to break that pattern of behavior. (Chapter 1)

■ Nonteams prevail in these situations for two basic reasons: (1) the single-leader mode of behavior works well most of the time, and (2) the prevailing mindset among senior leaders makes it virtually impossible for real teams to form. (Chapter 2)

■ Unexpected and near-crisis events occasionally produce real team efforts at the top, but they occur far too infrequently to exploit the potential for team, as well as nonteam, performance at the top. (Chapter 3)

■ Integrating two distinct disciplines that are normally in direct conflict—team and executive leadership—rather than compromising one for the other, is the key to greater leadership capacity within groups that run things at all levels. (Chapter 4)

■ Proactively identifying collective work products and unifying themes or initiatives can provide important catalysts for senior leadership groups that seek a better balance of team performance. (Chapter 5)

■ The capability to shift into and out of different modes of behavior and membership configurations is essential to increasing team performance at the top. (Chapter 6)

■ CEOs who can play multiple roles are more likely to achieve an optimal balance between team and nonteam performance within their top leadership group; however, they seldom need to change their basic individual leadership styles. (Chapter 7)

■ These lessons for "teams at the top" apply to teams that run things at virtually any level in the organization. (Chapter 8)

■ A balanced leadership approach at the top must be able to combine the essential individual leadership activities with the substantive collective work required for team performance. (Chapter 9)

The popular image of a "team at the top" is inconsistent with the context in which real teams work in high-performance companies. Teams are only one of several approaches that leaders apply in their pursuit of higher performance. Structures, processes, and informal networks are also important. The best senior leadership groups are learning to fit team performance—both at the top and elsewhere in the organization—into that context. Discipline, alignment, and balance are the themes of that context, not teams.

When all is said and done, it helps to know when to be concerned (or when to feel guilty!) about whether your senior leadership group is working as a real team or not—and what to do about it. There is little doubt that a significant number of senior executives and CEOs become frustrated that their top team efforts are so problematic. They sense the missed performance opportunity but resist the time and accountability tradeoff. Of most concern, perhaps, is that they see few performance gains from their efforts to be more teamlike. Equally disturbing is their recognition that the rest of the organization is aware of their predominantly nonteam behavior.

This book addresses those concerns directly. My position is that it can often be frustrating, pointless, and even counterproductive to try to force a group of top executives to become a team. However, there are some identifiable occasions and compelling reasons when a top team effort is essential in order to capture performance potential. The wisdom, if you will, is to differentiate between team and nonteam opportunities, and then shift into whichever mode is best for the task at hand. The inherent messages herein also have value to those readers who have been struggling with their disappointment about top teams. This book is intended for them, too, because it goes straight to the heart of that problem and what to do about it.

To that end, the book ends with "Diagnostic Guide: Obtaining Team Performance When It Counts" (Appendix C), for CEOs and other top leaders who seek to improve the leadership capacity and performance capability of their senior leadership groups. You need not perpetuate the plight of the creatures in the ancient Haida canoe who only row to the cadence of a single leader.

CHAPTER ONE

A Tougher Game at the Top

CHAMPION INTERNATIONAL CORPORATION was an early pioneer in the development of team-based "people systems" for running the company's paper mills, as well as its forest resources and forest product mills. It all began in the early 1980s, when Andrew Sigler and Robert Longbine agreed to build a state-of-the-art mill in Quinnesec, Michigan. State of the art came to include more than machine technology, however, and Quinnesec emerged as the centerpiece of CEO Sigler's long-range strategy of investing heavily in big machines and team-based "people systems" to transform the company into a stronger competitor. It has proven to be a long, hard journey in more ways than one.

The aspiration was simple enough: become the low-cost producer of quality paper for the markets in which they compete. Unfortunately, that aspiration was shared by most of the company's major competitors who could also afford to build "big machines." As a result, the differentiating factor in Sigler's mind became Champion's people systems rather than its machines. This was to be a set of management and operations systems wherein members of the workforce at the mills would be committed to the highest productivity, yield, and quality results. To make a long story short, this meant (to Sigler and Longbine at least) real teams running the mills. In those days, this was not exactly the application of proven best practices; rather, it was a highly risky and largely unproven approach.

Champion's quest for team performance eventually spanned dozens of mills and nine long years. It also encompassed numerous staff and support groups, such as finance and accounting services. There were many stops, starts, and stumbles along the way, any number of which would have discouraged most senior leadership groups from continuing. Thanks to Sigler's determination and the convictions of several of his executives, Champion "stayed the course" despite the many storms. Although today's top management views the journey as still under way, most of the mills and staff support groups have been literally transformed, technologically and culturally. As a result, the company now has several of the best mills in the industry in terms of quality and productivity. In 1995 the international technology consulting firm of Jaakko Poyry, which benchmarks worldwide paper mill performance, rated Champion's mills in Quinnesec, Michigan, and Brazil as among the very best in the world.

Somewhat surprisingly, perhaps, it took another four or five years beyond the mill transformations for team performance to penetrate the senior leadership group of the company. Why was it such a long, hard climb for team performance to reach the top? Largely because team performance at the top was less obviously necessary and more difficult to attain.

This chapter is a synopsis of Champion's decade-long pursuit of team performance—starting at the mills and moving up the line to the top. It is a story of both successes and failures over several years. It also illustrates why team performance down the line does not translate easily into team performance at the top. Most importantly, it demonstrates how valuable and difficult it can be to obtain team performance, as well as how different that game is at the top. The story covers three different leadership eras since 1984:

Era 1. Pioneering teams in the mills and staff support groups

Era 2. Transitioning to a new "team at the top"

Era 3. Pursuing Sigler's team legacy at the top

ERA 1: PIONEERING TEAMS IN THE MILLS

An industrial paper mill is no place for the faint of heart, the quiet mannered, or the sensitive. It is a cacophony of frightening noises and rumbling machinery, with huge logs rolling, sliding, and shifting about in seemingly uncontrolled chaos, and tough mill workers screaming orders at each other. The first time you walk through a mill, you fear for your own life, if not for the lives of those who seem to know what they are doing. A mill obviously requires a cadre of paper-making veterans who have learned their roles the hard way, know what they are doing, and can somehow make sense of the chaos. Most importantly, they instinctively know when a seemingly obscure noise, unobtrusive movement, or lack thereof demands quick corrective action. There is no time here for consensus management.

Mistakes in this chaotic milieu of people, machines, computers, logs, pulp, and water are both costly and dangerous. Accidents hurt people and performance, as well as pride. It's no wonder that traditional paper mills remained under the control of clear, strong hierarchies for more than a century. No one in his or her right mind would tamper with this Paul Bunyan version of controlled chaos without a pretty compelling reason. Even the likes of Andrew Sigler and Robert Longbine were at first reluctant when several of their best leaders pressed them to turn critical elements of production over to something called "self-directed work teams."

By 1985, however, the quest for teams at the mills had become a strategic imperative in Sigler's mind, not a noble search for some new, experimental paradigm of organization. Moreover, the paper industry at that time was hardly the place you went in search of teams. It was a relentless commodity business with unpredictably painful cycles of over- and undercapacity, which continue to dismay investors to this day. Success in this industry was as much a function of timber holdings, market position, and lucky timing as anything else. As Mike Corey, senior vice president of corporate analysis, describes it, "Overall profitability in this industry is heavily, if not primarily, determined by the wood segments [resources and markets] that you participate in—those are once or twice in a lifetime decisions."[1]

As a result, it has been very difficult, if not impossible, for large paper companies to materially change their relative financial performance without a major restructuring of their asset base (the location of their timberlands and wood sources) and their market position (where and how their products are distributed). Such changes have huge investment implications. On a worldwide scale, the prevailing monetary exchange rates can easily affect returns as much as or more than most other factors. Within that set of relatively unalterable strategic and economic constraints, the operating performance of the mills emerges as the primary management target for optimizing results. It was within that context that Sigler's strategy of investing in the most advanced paper-making machines and team-based mill management systems was framed.

A Difficult Strategy to Implement

Getting teams to run paper mills in those days, however, was not as simple as it sounds today. They were traditionally managed within a formal hierarchy controlled by a strong mill manager. As Sigler recalls, "Then the mills were run by old-line managers who had to control the workers and fend off the union; teams were practically unheard of."[2]

In fact, the mill managers—aptly characterized as "local CEOs"—were the product of a long tradition of single-leader discipline. In addition to being dedicated to their ensconced hierarchies, mill managers were also uniquely powerful and influential in their communities. Often the mill was the major, if not the only, employer in town. As a result, any significant shift to teams in the workplace invariably required replacement of the mill manager, who could not change his leadership approach enough to accommodate teams. But changing the mill manager was only the first step along a more complicated path of developing completely new skills and behavior patterns within the workforce. Shift foremen, machine operators, maintenance people, even storeroom and cleanup workers did their jobs within the tight constraints of prescribed processes and rules. They expected to be told what to do and when to do it—and they were expected to comply. It was a command-and-control culture that made sense to people at all levels.

Steve Goerner was the first of several "mill manager pioneers" to emerge in the Champion change saga. Although he was an experienced operations and engineering manager from the old school, that pattern had been broken by a stint in the construction and startup of a new plant in Brazil. He had also spent a year studying the latest in pulp-making technology and innovative people systems in a variety of industries. As a result, Sigler and Longbine naturally turned to Goerner to lead the experimental effort in the company's new site at Quinnesec, Michigan.

With strong support from the top, Goerner launched what was to become one of the first strongly team-based mill operating systems in the industry. The entire 620-person operation was organized around dozens of teams, supported by a management structure that emphasized team support and leadership. Teams were used wherever the collective work products seemed to justify it, and many of them took over what had previously been the exclusive domain of a hierarchical or single-leader management structure.

Adopting this kind of approach was not an easy transformation, but it has been surprisingly successful. Champion's workplace and staff support teams today are among the better examples of applying the basic elements required for real team levels of performance (summarized in Appendix B). Although not all of the early mill teams worked as anticipated, the new plant management system at Quinnesec provided the evidence that Sigler and Longbine needed to expand the approach to the rest of the Champion mills. Still, it was an unpopular, high-risk strategy—and many outside observers and analysts were predicting its failure.

By and large, however, the naysayers were wrong. There is little question today that the company's high-risk investment in team systems has paid off in operating and staff performance capability. Champion legitimately claims some of the best mill operating results in the industry. No one in the company and few in the industry would seriously question the value added by their mill and staff support teams. More than one outside analyst has been moved to acknowledge "the fundamental improvements in Champion's business [that] are still very much under-appreciated by a market caught up in history."

Unfortunately, during most of the early years there was little evidence that the improvement in mill operating capabilities was finding its way to the bottom line—quite the opposite, in fact. For years, outside observers and analysts have focused harsh attention on the company's erosion of shareholder wealth. Investor and analyst demands for better short-term results invariably prompted Sigler to explain that his strategy was a long-term one. He had no intention of tampering with it just to satisfy the barracudas on Wall Street, who periodically criticized Champion for underperforming the industry and perpetuating stock values that lagged both the market and the competition. Only within two of the last ten years did Champion's financial results gain words of respect from the analysts:

The company has focused on building a strong, efficient work force, recruiting and training to upgrade skills. . . . [It has] also given more responsibility which improved commitment and performance. . . . Productivity [tons per employee] is up 35 percent and costs down 12 to 14 percent.[3]

Obviously, this is not a business for those who seek short-term miracles or overnight fortunes. And even those who are in it over the long haul have trouble achieving respectable returns for shareholders. They have to build position and capability during the extended price depressions when the analysts strongly prefer cost and asset base reductions. Rightly or wrongly, Champion's "team at the top" believed this challenge required that it build a fundamental and unique mill capability *before* it could successfully attempt bold strategic restructuring and repositioning.

At the same time, Sigler realized that it would take more than teams running efficient paper mills to have an impact on overall company performance. Nor is there much doubt today that Champion's future performance aspirations will require bold strategic moves, particularly in international arenas, as well as the continued development of its superior mill operating capabilities. Simply put, the company's most critical performance challenges are moving up the line—which would seem to argue for being able to access the flexible, responsive, and diverse leadership capacity provided by real team efforts at the top.

Champion's overall financial record over the past ten years, however, is not the point of this case, nor is it relevant to the company's team performance experience, either at the mills or within the senior leadership group. It would be naive on my part to attempt to explain or correlate overall company returns with team performance at either place, simply because of the multitude of other factors that determine overall corporate results. It is possible, however, to learn a great deal from the company's team experience, which is clearly better than most at several levels over an extended period of time. Few companies can match its experience and record of team performance.

A Different Approach up the Line

Performance issues above the level of the mills and the staff support groups have only recently been addressed by real teams. Nor was much thought given to pursuing team approaches among the senior corporate leadership group during the several difficult years of mill transformations. Even in organizations like Champion, where front-line teams are proven performers, comparable efforts become increasingly elusive the closer you get to the top, often requiring more than one generation of leadership before they can be realized. Like the traditional mill managers described earlier, strong CEOs are not natural team leaders.

Andrew Sigler was no exception. In fact, he was the classic model of a strong and disciplined executive leader at the top—so strong that he could easily intimidate any and all of his direct reports, particularly in group sessions. Those who worked with him over time, however, recognized and respected the fact that his intimidating comments usually had a constructive purpose. It was simply his way of keeping the group focused on the practical realities of the issue under discussion. In one-on-one sessions, he could be much less formidable, if not charming and sensitive. As a result, everybody in Champion's top management ranks learned that confronting Sigler in a group session was far less likely to work than confronting him in private.

He made his mark at Champion in the marketing side of the business. Joining the company as a salesman in 1956, he quickly stood out from the crowd, both physically and managerially. Close to six and a half feet tall, he could easily pass for a professional basketball player. He not only towered over most people in the company, he also had a booming voice and spoke with an aura of authority and conviction that commanded attention and respect. It was virtually impossible for Sigler to be part of any group without being presumed to be its leader. He learned much of his executive leadership discipline as a pilot in Korea; he flew several combat missions and then returned to work for Champion. From the beginning, Sigler was a natural leader at the company, and it came as no surprise when he was named CEO at the age of 42 in 1974. His predecessor had lasted only 18 months, largely because of the board's growing concern with what had been referred to as a "haphazard diversification drive."

Sigler was anything but haphazard. From day one, he focused relentlessly on improving the core paper business, despite its cyclical challenges. His "team at the top" was always a small one, and there was never any doubt as to who was its leader. For the 20-plus years that Sigler, with Bob Longbine (and later Whitey Heist) as COO and Ken Nichols as CFO, ran the company, they operated primarily as a working group, or nonteam—despite the fact that many of those years were devoted to the development of real team performance in the mills. They were masters of what I call the "single-leader working group" or "executive leadership discipline"; this is common at the top of most well-run companies and is summarized in the box below. Not surprisingly, most of the traditional mill managers that Champion's new people systems displaced had been experienced practitioners of this discipline as well. And that is a good part of the reason why virtually all of them had to be replaced in order for the team-based mill approaches to flourish. As Mark Childers, the senior Champion

EXECUTIVE LEADERSHIP DISCIPLINE

1. *Create and maintain urgency.* Build a true sense of urgency about increasing performance results in the unit or units for which individual leaders are responsible.

2. *Resolve the critical strategic issues.* Formulate a clear, compelling corporate strategy; identify and focus unrelenting attention on the resolution of the most critical strategic issues.

3. *Enforce individual accountability.* Establish clear individual accountability for all executives and managers; reward or punish managers in accordance with their individual results.

4. *Leverage executive time.* Leverage executive time and experience through efficient organization and management processes; give high-potential leaders responsibility for increasing numbers of people and assets.

5. *Make the tough decisions individually.* Hold individual executives clearly responsible for making the critical decisions in their primary areas of responsibility, and track the results of those decisions in evaluating their performance.

6. *Pick the best individuals for the key jobs.* Develop superior judgment as a leader in evaluating the potential of others against a strong template of individual leadership and performance capability.

7. *Periodically raise the bar.* Strive for earnings growth and improvement each year, not only for the company but also for each manager; promote people based on individual performance results as well as potential.

executive who helped develop this case, points out, "none of the old mill managers remain."

Why Single-Leader Discipline Prevails

Unfortunately, world-class teams at the front line do not naturally lead to team performance up the line—particularly at the top—for a number of very good reasons. As was the case at Champion, senior executives work long and hard to get to the top—and seldom has that effort required, or even included, real team behaviors on their part. The traditional patterns of individual accountability and responsibility that senior leaders master to reach the top become very deeply ingrained. They become accustomed to calling any small group effort "a team," even though most of those efforts are driven by strong individual leaders who do not apply team discipline. In fact, it is almost heresy to suggest that individual accountability might be complemented by the mutual accountability of teams.

It is invariably easier and more comfortable for senior executives to operate within a clear hierarchy, where single-leader discipline prevails. Consequently, successful single-leader units are much more common at the top, and team efforts are difficult to find within most of those senior leadership approaches. Part of the problem is that most people do not know how or where to look for team performance within those models—even though unexpected crises and other major events will produce team behavior at the top (Chapter 3 is devoted to this phenomenon). Nonetheless, it is rare and takes place mostly behind closed doors, out of view of the rest of the organization.

Additionally, the discipline required for team results is considerably more difficult to apply at the top. It is often in direct conflict with the discipline required for strong executive performance. Top executives are dedicated to the principles of individual accountability and consequence management; team disciplines demand mutual accountability and collective work among team members. These are not natural bedfellows.

Perhaps the most difficult aspect of applying team discipline at the top is dealing with the expectations of others. Many of the people who pay convincing lip service to teams at the top are really very nervous about environments that are not protected by a strong single leader. Mark Childers refers to this as "the need for someone to make a clearing in the forest." Most people in a large company undergoing significant change can easily be overwhelmed by the complexities and potential chaotic confusion around them. They struggle with the insecurities thus created and look to a strong leader to clear it all up—or at least to clear away enough of the underbrush to allow them to do their job. Take away the strong leader, and you take away their primary source of protection, who, they believe, can really "make a clearing in the forest." Like it or not, any suggestion of real team behavior at the top implies just the opposite.

As a result, few executives take the trouble to differentiate a real team from a single-leader–driven work group. Typically, they avoid the issue by referring to any small group activity as a "team effort," thereby preserving the notion of teamwork without having to take the risks of mutual accountability and shared or shifting leadership. Even companies, like Champion, that master team approaches elsewhere in their organization have a difficult time with real team efforts at the top.

Increasingly, however, Sigler and Heist recognized the difficult paradox they knew they must address: a single-leader discipline at the top would not be good enough to leverage mill team operating performance into overall company performance. Strategic issues and broad leadership challenges above the mills cried out for team, as well as individual, performance. But it was not until the next generation of leadership took over that the senior executives were able to function in any kind of a real team capacity. Only then did they develop real team norms, working styles, and shared understanding of the elements of team discipline to a point where they could shift out of their natural working group behavior patterns and function as a real team. More importantly, they also learned when and how to shift back to a single-leader unit without feeling guilty!

ERA 2: THE LEADERSHIP TRANSITION

Like many other real team efforts at the top, it took a major event to bring the senior leadership team opportunity into full focus at

Champion. In this case, the event was an unexpected decision by Sigler and Heist to retire simultaneously. Their purpose was to transition the top leadership roles clearly and cleanly to the next generation. As a result, Sigler in particular became focused on the need for a special "transition process" to broaden the groups' leadership skills and enable more team performance at the top.

In the first place, it was not obvious when this transition would occur, because Sigler had not decided himself. Nor was it obvious that the two senior leaders should retire at the same time, as they were not the same age. Certainly, it was not obvious who the successor should be, because a simultaneous retirement meant that Heist was not to be a candidate. Some members of the board believed it would be necessary to go to the outside. This option was doubly appealing because of the perpetual difficulty of delivering consistent financial performance and the apparent absence of anyone with Sigler's strong grasp of strategic issues. Sigler and Heist, on the other hand, were convinced that the continuing nourishment of team approaches in the mills and elsewhere would require top leadership that truly comprehended the significance, performance potential, and sensitivity of their workplace teams. Recruiting a CEO from outside the company without this perspective was, in their view, much too big a risk. More importantly, they also believed that more than one of the next generation of executives had the potential to lead the company—particularly if the successor could retain the support of the others, thereby adding real team capability to the senior leadership mixture.

Roughly two years prior to Sigler's target retirement date, the transition became the top-priority item on his and Heist's leadership agenda. They envisioned a process that would not only facilitate a smooth transition at the very top, but also better capitalize on the kind of team capability and commitment at the top that the company was increasingly experiencing down the line. Sigler, in fact, had been convinced for some time that real team performance within the senior leadership group could not occur until he and Heist were "out of the way." Old habits and expectations would not give way to team discipline until the cast of characters changed.

In most companies, this issue might have been viewed as a matter of simply picking the right successor and reorganizing a new top structure around that individual (the common definition of "team at the top"). Sigler and Heist were convinced, however, that unless the solution could also ensure a more cohesive, real team capability among the top half-dozen or so leaders, the company would miss a major opportunity in creating new leadership capacity, flexibility, and responsiveness for the future.

A Separate Leadership Transition Process

To that end, Sigler launched a separate leadership process, involving the 18 members of his senior leadership group in a series of regular meetings and working sessions. To his board and other outside observers, he described the process simply as a way of helping determine his successor. In his own mind, however, it was the best way to accelerate the development of broader team capability and leadership capacity within the group. This process had two important dimensions: (1) building the group's strategic knowledge of the business and industry (because Sigler, Heist, and Nichols had always provided that) and (2) strengthening the group's ability to work in different team configurations among themselves. He also knew, however, how difficult it would be for others—particularly the board—to understand this purpose as readily as they would understand the more common notion of simply "picking a successor." Sigler had his hands full convincing others that the process was more important than the solutions. The senior leadership group was looking for the organizational answer at first, whereas the board kept seeking a single-successor answer. Despite these pressures for "an answer," Sigler and Heist patiently kept the process in the forefront.

It is a simple process to describe. A series of special meetings was scheduled off site at Champion's Treetop facility near the Stamford, Connecticut, headquarters. The setting was important because it took the senior group away from operating interruptions and provided a more open working atmosphere than their normal management meetings in the office. The agenda evolved into a combination of strategic, leadership, and organization topics that enabled the group to go well beyond the issues they could address within existing management processes. The working approach for the new process was one of informal and open discussion, seeded by subgroup and individual work between the meetings. Most of the time, in the view of Richard Olson (current CEO), they functioned as single-leader working groups with assignments determined by Sigler.

At one point early on, the group directly addressed the question: Should we (the entire 18-person group) be functioning more as a team and less as a working group? Nearly everyone agreed with Sigler that they should continue in their "working group" mode because: (1) all 18 members needed to be involved in the process, and that was too large and diverse a group to shape into a single team, and (2) it was much too late for Sigler and Heist to change their strong individual styles and single-leader roles to allow real team behaviors—except perhaps in subgroups. Simply put, the expectations of others, as well as their own habit patterns, would not allow it within any realistic time frame.

The subgroups soon became a very important element of the process, and a few of them functioned as real teams. For example, a group of five or six executives worked as a team in addressing key strategic issues. Bill Birchfield and Tom Terfehr led an effort to address performance opportunities in purchasing and materials, which spawned a number of subteams. Joe Donald led an effort to spread best manufacturing practices throughout the company. The small groups worked in both team and working group modes, depending on what the situation demanded. They also benefited from their "report-back" interactions with the entire senior group, which served to reinforce their goals and enrich their perspective and information base.

While the "committee of the whole" was never a real team, it became a powerful learning and communication forum that was integral to the transition process over the two-year period. Most importantly in Olson's view, the additional working exposure to other future team members probably sped up the process of building trust and understanding. Certainly, Sigler's role in this group was different at the end than in the beginning (the evolution of this role is described in more detail in Chapter 7), as the group became more cohesive, open, and focused in its efforts. It also became more effective in shaping subteam efforts as appropriate. Although never a real team of 18, the group members were learning team behaviors in their interactions that would enable them to extend their team performance at the top after the transition.

Of course, the critical decision on a CEO successor was wrapped up in the process. To Sigler's credit, he was able to keep it from becoming central to the agenda or overly disruptive to the senior group's working approach. He remained convinced that the most important issue was not the choice of his successor, but the capacity of that successor to enable real team behaviors within the emerging new senior leadership group. Probably the most important priority of his two-year transition process was achieving that end—it was his legacy of team performance at the top.

ERA 3: PURSUING THE LEGACY

When Richard E. Olson was named to succeed Sigler as CEO in the spring of 1996, no one was more surprised than Dick himself. He had expected that several others were likely to be chosen, and he would have been more than supportive of any of them. Nonetheless, he was fully confident that, with the kind of team support they had already begun, he could lead the company to new levels of performance. His immediate first steps, therefore, were aimed at coalescing his colleagues into the kind of group that could perform as a real team whenever the situation called for it. He and Nichols spent many hours in deliberations about "the process," which early on was focused on the newly emerging senior leadership group. Nichols remembers the early sessions most clearly:

> The first executive meetings after Sigler's announcement were awkward as hell. There was still some lingering emotion about Sigler's choice from those who felt passed over. And because Andy was still around, he was still telling people what to do. . . . The transition was hard for Andy, who was uncomfortable being out of the loop and the decision-making role. Dick would give periodic updates, especially on the reorganization, but it damn near killed Andy. The team capacity of the group was definitely strengthened after the retirements took effect.

Olson, of course, not only had the advantage of being the new leader on the block, he also had a natural style that was more team-friendly.

His attitude was basically: One of us cannot be as good as all of us working together. He was much more patient and willing than most to let his colleagues wallow around a bit "to find a common language" and understand each other's diverse views before seeking a decision. "It was important to allow time for the group to explore the different meanings that different members attach to certain key thoughts and terms." He was also more comfortable encouraging, coaching, and enabling others to lead the group. At the same time, he wasn't reluctant to make decisions himself or to force directions on the group members whenever their interactions reached a point of diminishing returns— either because an answer became obvious or because conflicting views appeared unlikely to merge through further group debate. Like most natural team leaders, he sought the best decision, not necessarily a consensus.

Learning More About Each Other

The size of the group changed materially (dropping from 18 to 8), as the transition process indicated it should. This "Gang of 8" (as they now refer to themselves) included the former heads of the major lines of business and key staff leaders. Comprised mostly of Olson's and Nichols's direct reports, it's a more natural team grouping than before. Yet it does not always function as a team. For example, the group worked diligently in different configurations over the summer months in 1996 to create a new organization plan that would better align decisions and actions with strategic as well as operational priorities— and that could better capitalize on the emerging team capabilities. However, Nichols is quick to point out that only during the next phase of this reorganizing effort—that of designing and staffing second level positions, forums, and processes—did the entire Gang of 8 function as a real team. The initial establishment of the first-level positions and roles was basically Olson's decision, working closely with Nichols on the specifics. They involved the Gang of 8 primarily as a working group, led by Olson and Nichols in the final shaping, to ensure both understanding and support. Although not really a team decision, it did give members a chance to air their opinions and develop common commitment through information and opinion sharing. But it was a very different process than the group had been used to under Sigler. Nichols described some of his early frustrations as follows:

> We spent half a day around that table—and talked and talked and talked and talked. It nearly drove me nuts! I kept wanting to pound the table and say, "Let's just get on with it"—but [in retrospect] the prolonged discussion was very important to do because we were learning about each other. It was not just about the new structure, but about how each of us really thought and felt. . . . things we never recognized before—even though we had worked together for years. In my case, there is no question that I learned the value of listening longer, and not challenging people so quickly. I had not been giving [my colleagues] a chance to complete their ideas, many of which were really good ones. . . . I think others learned as well.

During one of their early working sessions in the fifteenth-floor boardroom, Sigler opened the door and looked in. Childers was drawing something on a flip chart and, through force of habit, stopped abruptly upon Sigler's entrance. Sigler took a long look around the room, smiled wryly, rolling his eyes in mock dismay, and left with the words "God help us!" It was clear that the game was no longer his to win or lose.

Unleashing Real Team Capacity

The first true team project for the Gang of 8 was to shape the organization specifics below the top level and to staff those lower management levels. In this session, Olson and Nichols did not come with preconceived notions beyond the new functional structure at the top. Thus everyone in the group not only presented opinions, but also problem-solved together about the best way to shape and staff all areas. It took several weeks and many working sessions before it all came together. In fact, the rest of the organization "got a bit antsy," in Nichols' words, as the actual announcement of the new approach was repeatedly delayed.

The group also worked as a real team in developing the "road show" program to announce and discuss the changing of the guard. The entire Gang of 8 worked on it, and five of the eight (Olson, Nichols, Twig

MacArthur, Donald, and Scott Barnard) ended up giving significant presentations. Sigler and Heist took a few minutes up front, but the show clearly belonged to the new team. Although Heist stayed for all of the initial session, Sigler "just wandered off" as it became clear the new team was running the show very well.

The Gang of 8 also learned that they could not delegate down without setting a cogent direction and set of principles—as a team. For example, early on, they commissioned a lower-level task force to work with a group of consultants to design a new compensation program that would better enable and reward collective accomplishments. The task force came back with a set of recommendations that did not satisfy what the Gang of 8 had in mind. Nichols argues that the effort was doomed before it began because the Gang of 8 had not agreed on or made clear their own goals and willingness to take risks. Olson recognized that the problem was not with the consultants, however. Instead of allowing a long debate about their recommendations, therefore, he decided to bring the topic back onto the senior team's agenda. They spent the better part of perhaps a dozen sessions over a three-month period working the problem as a team and came up with a solution that was much more on target. Interestingly, the compensation project was not the kind of project usually handled at the top. In this case, however, it was not only a critical issue, but also a natural "collective work product" for a real team effort.

A year into the new leadership approach, the senior group continues to function as the "Gang of 8"—sometimes in a real team mode, sometimes not. What is clearly different is how much time they actually spend working together on significant strategic and performance issues. They meet every Monday morning for two or three hours on longer-term issues, and again in the afternoon for normal operating matters. They also meet for most of the day every Friday to continue shaping their long-term aspirations, formulate overall corporate strategies and direction, and resolve critical issues. In some of these sessions, they are in a learning mode, with presentations by outside experts, consultants, investment bankers, and industry analysts. The group exhibits a very open, learning mindset, reflecting the high degree of trust that has developed among the members. This turns out to be typical of real team efforts at any level, as Harvard professor Richard Hackman's work on this topic indicates: "when in a learning mode, members were able to bootstrap themselves to greater skill and performance even when they encountered failures. . . . the capacity for learning was directly related to the amount of trust that existed among the members."[4]

Overall, it is clear that each member of the group feels extremely positive about the new leadership approach. Although it is much too soon to attach success or failure to their efforts, it is not too soon to note the differences that real team capability makes in their motivation, enthusiasm, and commitment. As Nichols puts it, "I can't wait to get to work every morning. . . . I never worked this hard and never enjoyed my work this much." This is not a trivial comment, coming as it does from someone whom his colleagues have for years recognized as the ultimate "executive workaholic."

The key differences between the newly emerging team at the top, and the Sigler/Heist single-leader working group approach are important to note:

- The Gang of 8 is a significantly smaller group, which can work more easily together in different modes of group behavior—sometimes as a team, sometimes not.

- Many of the members play more than one leadership role in different small-group configurations. Often the most senior person is *not* the leader.

- The role of the CEO is markedly different, as Olson is much more comfortable in a team leader role, yet takes charge when he needs to.

- The number of subteam efforts has expanded greatly, particularly above the mill level. The reorganization is very dependent on cross-functional business teams.

Because the Gang of 8 had come together so quickly and effectively, it became increasingly awkward for Sigler and Heist to remain involved, nor was it comfortable for the Gang to simply ignore them. Consequently, both Sigler and Heist left the company and the board in the fall of 1996—about three months ahead of schedule. As he had intended, Andrew Sigler had effectively accomplished his private mission of transitioning the leadership of the company to a group that he knew would increasingly achieve team levels of performance at the top, as well as in the mills. It may have been a long time coming, but it was a legacy that reflected his belief that team performance matters a lot—even at the top!

The View from Below

Team efforts below the top provide useful comparisons with and windows on the impact of the top team. To begin with, they are clearly influenced by what senior leaders say and do. Certainly the senior group under Sigler provided strong support and encouragement for teams below. More importantly perhaps, teams below can and do emulate senior leaders. Thus, when the new group at Champion went even further with its own real team actions and behaviors, this did not go unnoticed by teams down the line. The reorganization has created upwards of 20 new business-integrating or managing teams. The Gang of 8 actually designed the domestic pulp and paper business into what, on paper at least, looks like the old functional organization: mill operations under Joe Donald, sales under Scotty Barnard, and marketing under Twig MacArthur. Of course, the vertical functions in this case are overlaid with cross-functional business teams, creating what conventional wisdom would call a dysfunctional matrix. In the world of decentralized organization design and the rush to disaggregated business units, functional structures and matrix organizations might well be considered a step backward—unless you happen to believe in the power of cross-functional teams. Despite conventional wisdom, you only have to have a few discussions with any one of the Gang of 8 to become a believer yourself.

David Stubbs is the vice president of marketing for uncoated paper. He is part of a four-person team that manages the uncoated paper business, comprising about $1.2 billion in sales. It is typical of the several new business unit leadership teams that were created with the reorganization. These teams are launched, nourished, and supported by the Gang of 8 to ensure team performance and accountability. When first formed in 1996, organization development executives worked with each potential team to define the members' team roles versus their individual roles. For the first four to five months, the business teams communicated mostly on short-term issues, but rarely on strategic or longer-term issues. Increasingly, however, each team is taking more of the lead set by the Gang of 8. For example, Stubbs' team has started meeting every Monday and Friday to focus on longer-term issues. In addition, they meet once a month with a senior leadership subteam of Barnard, MacArthur, and Donald, to apprise them of the financials and discuss troublesome issues they are facing, explain new initiatives they are undertaking, and explore overall business trends.

Stubbs had actually left a headquarters job in 1989, so he had not been around during Sigler's last years. His impression was that people felt good about having Sigler giving clear direction about where the business was going or not going. Like Childers' earlier observation, Stubbs felt that the protection Sigler had provided by making a "clearing in the forest" had been important. When he moved back to headquarters during the latest reorganization, the clearing in the forest had disappeared with Sigler, and Dave found the first few months pretty chaotic. By the beginning of 1997, however, things had clearly stabilized a great deal, and people like Stubbs increasingly saw the top team coming together to focus on the key issues and opportunities. Most importantly, Stubbs now sees a "real and permanent evolution of the top team from 'telling and controlling' to 'listening and advising.'" Because he knew Joe Donald and Scott Barnard personally before the reorganization, he has been particularly impressed with how much they have been able to change their roles. "Scott and Joe like to have their hands in the middle of things and make the decisions themselves. . . . [Surprisingly] they've let that go." In this context, Stubbs sees the biggest challenge for the business unit leadership teams to be boldness in accepting the broader solution space within which the Gang of 8 now expects them to operate.

In the past, people waited to be told what to do. Now it's different—not unlike a dog that is constrained by an invisible [electronic] fence. You live for a long time with that fence around there. You know that if you go to this point you're going to get zapped and so you go back. Eventually, you don't go near there anymore. I think with us, we're now in a situation where we need to get used to the fact that we can now go out there beyond the old fence lines. And, once you go out there you need to be more comfortable knowing what you're doing when you're out there.

Olson makes a similar point with regard to the Gang of 8. He believes that "you really have to pull them over the line" that they have been used to staying behind. He recalls a close analogy from his past, when one of his mill teams resisted his invitation to determine for themselves how to change their mill organization. For several days, apparently, they sat around thinking, "Dick knows what he wants—why doesn't he just *tell* us what he wants?" When they finally realized that Dick really did not know what he wanted, and therefore really did expect them to determine how to organize the unit, Olson recalls that "they found it pretty scary. . . . I told them I found it scary too!" The same attitude was a problem at first within the Gang of 8.

Applying Team Discipline up the Line

With close to ten years of mill team experience to build on, you would think that the emerging senior leadership group would have few problems in shaping real team performance at the top. To some extent this has been true. In fact, Olson and Nichols both believe that the group's past experience with real teams down the line was perhaps more important than Sigler's special transition process in preparing the new senior group to hit the ground running with regard to team behaviors. Nonetheless, the task has not been particularly easy.

The real team game is different at the top largely because the discipline required for team performance is often in direct conflict with the discipline required for executive leadership. In fact, it is useful to recognize how a strong single-leader discipline like that which prevailed in Champion's old mill structure is in direct conflict with the strong discipline that is required for real team levels of performance, as defined in *Wisdom of Teams*.[5] (These conflicts are compared in more detail in Chapter 4.) At the mill level, Champion's senior leadership group intuitively recognized these conflicts and dealt with them, even though it meant replacing the mill managers. Within their own ranks, however, the urgency for change was less pressing. And, even though Sigler himself was well aware of the opportunity for team performance above the mills, he felt that the mill challenge must be addressed first. He also believed that changing his own patterns of behavior at that stage in the company's development would be more disruptive and confusing to both his board and his management group. The time was not right to risk those tradeoffs.

CONCLUSION: DIFFICULT LESSONS TO LEARN

The Champion story of team performance is unusual in several respects. First, it is one of the very few examples of a complete change in the culture as well as the performance capability of a large company. As such, it has taken over ten years to accomplish—and was heavily dependent on strong executive leadership discipline at the top. Second, the groundbreaking work with teams at the mills created a remarkable base of team experience and knowledge, which strongly influenced team efforts at the top as well as the operating performance of the mills. Third, the future performance of the company will depend as much on major strategic adjustments as on mill operating performance. The new leadership group must deal with both, and its relative success will ultimately be a function of both. As a result, team performance at the top will become much more important in the future. Admittedly, it is tempting to suggest—but impossible to support—the hypothesis that real team efforts at the top were late in coming. The simple fact that the mills were run by teams, while the company was not, can hardly explain a complex issue like overall company performance in the paper industry.

Nonetheless, if you ask the Gang of 8 today, most will tell you unequivocally that, if the senior leadership group could have functioned more as it does now, it would have made a difference in overall company performance. However, Olson probably speaks for most of the group when he says, "There is little doubt in my mind that we could have come a lot closer to being a premier company (and still can!!) by working more often as a real team at the top; it is also clear that *there is no way we could have done it before now!* [emphasis added]"

Obviously, the jury is still out on Champion's new leadership group. There is a clear need to bring collective power, flexibility, discipline, and leadership capacity to bear on the increasingly tough and critical strategic issues that will determine Champion's future performance and position in the industry. Only time will tell how well those in the new leadership group will be able to meet that challenge. One thing is certain, however. They will not be attempting it without having an arsenal that includes both executive leadership and team performance discipline at the top.

CHAPTER TWO

Why "Nonteams" Prevail at the Top

THE TEAM IS A SIMPLE, proven performance unit. Disciplined teams continue to penetrate the front line, the cross-functional middle ranks, and special task force efforts at all levels, at dozens, if not hundreds, of companies. Yet we find little evidence of real teams penetrating senior leadership groups or so-called teams at the top. Despite the increasing value of team performance down the line, nonteam behaviors continue to prevail at the top. This paradox is not easy to explain.

Is it because real teams are too simple to fit the complex challenges facing top executives, or too diversionary for the demanding, urgent issues that top leaders must address? Is it because executive priorities and egos preclude team behavior? Do real teams simply not work under the conditions top executives face?

It is abundantly clear that nonteams work, particularly at the top. There is a natural order to things; it tends to be hierarchical. Place 11 guinea hens in a pen, and science tells us that they will instinctively sort out a natural pecking order. This establishes which hen is strongest, the accepted ranking among them, and who influences whom. In human organizations as well, it is important to establish who reports to whom and who is in charge of what. These are reasonable things to want to know, and knowing the answers helps everyone get things done in a large institution.

Leadership groups at the top of human organizations are a bit more complicated than simple animal analogies imply. Nonetheless, the same instincts for strong, individual leadership persist. Most of us prefer strong leaders who will shoulder the burden of "making a clearing in the forest" that ensures organizational performance and helps sustain the viability of the institution against the unpredictable forces at work in our society. The value and security we gain from a strong leader is undeniable, and team behavior often seems to threaten both.

Teams are more likely to disrupt the natural order of things at the top. They do not sustain established, predictable patterns of leadership or respect time-honored rules and roles for the members. They are neither efficient nor orderly groupings. Seldom are they the best way to get normal work accomplished or routine problems solved. Although they may protect their members, they do not follow comfortable pathways, nor do they maintain a predictable pecking order based on the relative formal positions of the members. Moreover, teams are seldom the fastest way for a group with an experienced, capable leader to "get where they are going," particularly if the leader has been there before. And teams certainly require long hours of hard work!

It is no wonder that most leadership groups at the top of large and successful organizations function mostly as "nonteams." It is somewhat curious, however, that we persist in calling them "teams at the top." It is even more curious that the behavior they exhibit is perceived to be "unteamly"—most of the time. The reason, of course, is because the term *team* is used in casual conversation to describe a wide variety of different group interactions. Since I will be referring to many of these, the reader may find it useful to refer to the Glossary of Team Terms used in this book (Appendix A). Increasingly, the careless use of team labels and language contributes to a lack of rigor and discipline in identifying team opportunities and applying the discipline of team basics. Thus it can be very worthwhile to "clean up our language" on teams.

There is no denying that teams have worked for hundreds of years— and, every now and then, we do find one at the top. A real team is not some kind of temporary organizational fad promulgated by new-paradigm gurus; *teams are here to stay.* It is hard to believe, therefore, that they are not of more value at the top. I am convinced that the answer is not more undisciplined teams at the top, however. It is a more discriminating application of the basic elements of team discipline. There are two basic reasons why team discipline is not more broadly and consistently applied among senior leadership groups:

1. The basic elements of the team discipline (Appendix B) are considerably less clear, if not more difficult to apply, at the top.

2. Top executives are more naturally comfortable in a nonteam mode.

LESS CLEAR APPLICATION OF TEAM DISCIPLINE

The application of the discipline is different at the top—and usually more difficult. Mark Childers captured the essence of the difference in a simple phrase—"Things are a lot grayer at the top." To better understand what he meant by "grayness" and what it implies at the top, we asked Childers and Mike Corey to describe how the mill teams work (at both mill management and front-line levels). The contrast is instructive with respect to how a team at the top must think differently about applying each of the basic elements of the team discipline (size, skills, purpose, goals, working approach, and accountability, as summarized in Appendix B).[1] Childers cites the Sartell mill as a good example of mill management teams.

At Sartell, three management teams run the actual operations. Each team is comprised of people from the machines, pulp mills, wood yard, and finishing; there may also be representatives from utilities and maintenance on the team. Each team is responsible for the mill product (quality, quantity, cost, and productivity). The team consists of 17 people, including the mill manager and 8 union representatives.

The management team meets every morning to discuss previous performance, the day's operational needs, and any problems (such as the need to shut down a machine for maintenance). In addition, the full leadership team meets about twice a month to discuss longer-term issues, such as new product development, organizational issues, and machine outages or major rebuilds. And the team makes joint decisions on how to allocate capital between the different operations. This means that each member brings a "wish list" and then the team members jointly prioritize the needs based on the overall operation. Managers also meet informally during the day to resolve any current operational questions or problems.

Their purpose as a group is to maximize mill performance, and their team role constitutes a full-time job. Their goals stem from that purpose, and each set of mill teams has overall goals in terms of productivity, safety, quality, tonnage, environment, and people development. The managers' performance is evaluated both individually and as part of the team. The skills match the requirements of their role. For example, paper machine managers are experts and critical to all decisions involving the machine operations. Finally, accountability is collectively assumed by all members, based on the very explicit, but subjective KPIs (key performance indicators) for the mill overall.

Mike Corey helped with a similar picture of the front-line teams and also compared how the front line used to work before the team systems were put in place. The machine teams are even more clearly focused than the management teams, and their behaviors and attitudes are very different from those of the old mill system. For example, before the conversions to team systems, each person's sense of purpose was entirely individual—to do his or her specific job. Correspondingly, the manager's sense of purpose was to see that customer orders were met. Now the entire team sees its common purpose as satisfying customer needs while maximizing quality and productivity. This purpose is a more collective one, but it is still crystal clear. It also comprises the primary job responsibility for each team member.

The same is true with performance goals. Before the mills converted to teams, the goal was to meet daily customer orders and produce tons—period. Under the team system, there are key performance indicators (KPIs) above and beyond just meeting orders. These KPIs lead to goals in environment, productivity, safety, quality, and organization development. Each member of the team is clear on these goals. Before the team approach, the manager would give orders to everybody and simply make sure his orders were followed. Operators focused only on their own specific assignments, not on the machine's overall operations. "Guys in the pulp mills simply did not talk to guys on the paper machines." Now they all work together to maximize their machine's output relative to its earlier performance and the machine's potential. Because the members work together for long periods (several months, sometimes years), they are able to tailor their approaches to each other's working patterns. Most importantly, they also develop the ability to listen to each other and collaborate for problem solving and crisis resolution.

In some mills, before teams, mill managers would make subjective decisions on an individual's performance, whereas now all team members hold themselves mutually accountable for the team's performance. In addition to individual performance measurement based on skill levels, the mill leadership team members are compensated on objective measures of performance (based on the KPIs cited above), total mill performance, and overall Champion performance.

At both mill manager and front-line levels, there is more clarity about each of the elements of team discipline. Although the team approach introduces a more collective mindset than in the previous mill system of individual accountability, the teams are still relatively simple and straightforward. As team efforts approach the top of the organization, however, Childers' notion of "a greater degree of grayness" starts to become apparent, and the degree of grayness increases with each higher level of team behavior. The following sections explore how this occurs within each of the critical elements of the discipline required for team performance: purpose, goals, skills, working approach, and mutual accountability.

A Meaningful Purpose Is More Elusive

Real teams at any level must be deeply committed to a purpose that is very meaningful to each and every member—a purpose that goes well beyond the tangible accomplishments of the team. The purpose not only provides a sense of direction to the members, it also justifies the extra levels of effort each must make to achieve real team levels of performance. A truly meaningful purpose strengthens and sharpens the team's focus and commitment over time. To that end, it is periodically shaped and reshaped by the team, in a process sometimes referred to as "purposing."

At the mill level, Champion's front-line work teams had little trouble articulating a meaningful purpose related to the output of their specific machine base (such as running a paper machine at Sartell at its optimal capacity). These purposes usually pertain to the capacity of the machine and the ultimate quality of the product relative to customer specifications. The mill management teams' purpose was to maximize mill performance as defined by their KPIs. The purpose for Dave

Stubbs' business unit team (described in Chapter 1) was based on their product line: to improve the profitability and long-term market position in uncoated paper products. In all three cases, the purpose constitutes *the* major part of their job.

The purpose of a team effort at the top is not nearly as easy to articulate. It does not tie to a machine or a single product line, nor does it constitute the major job activity of the members of the senior leadership group. Top team efforts are more likely to be part-time. Childers' notion of "more grayness" seems to capture this difference. At one level of abstraction, the purpose of the team at the top is easily identified as "improve company performance" or "implement the company strategy." Unfortunately, that all-encompassing level of abstraction is much too broad to provide adequate focus or accountability for a real team effort by a small group.

The challenge is to wisely narrow or sharpen the focus from the overall company purpose to one or more supporting purposes, which can serve as a clear focal point for a small group's accomplishment and mutual accountability. For example, the senior leadership group at Champion was eventually able to develop subteam efforts around specific issues and tasks (purchasing and materials handling, strategy formulation, organization design) whose purposes were explicit enough to warrant real team efforts. A team purpose that addresses these kinds of issues, however, is not as easy to evolve as one that optimizes machine output. And, because it is a bit grayer than the more specific output and quality purpose at the mill, it provides a less-compelling rationale for team behaviors and accountability. Simply put, a "meaningful purpose" differs for teams at the top because it is

- Invariably confused with the overall corporate mission.
- Difficult to frame in ways that ensure small-group accountability, both individual and mutual.
- Chosen from a much wider range of alternative purposes.

The Performance Goals Are Less Tangible

The most obvious requirement for real team performance is a set of clear, measurable performance goals. Unfortunately, the problem of "grayness" comes into play again at the top. With the front-line teams the goals are clear, specific, recurring, and measurable. They deal with machine running rates, downtime, changeover speeds, yield, costs, and overall output. These become second nature to teams running the machines, and the goals they set are simple extensions of a set of very tangible measures of productivity and quality. Dave Stubbs' business unit teams simply set joint goals based on the financial and operating performance drivers; for example, increase the product mix to include 20 percent value-added products.

At the top, however, the small group goals are more elusive and often less tangible. Appropriate team goals must be culled out of corporate targets, as well as line-of-business, long-term financial, market share, and individual executive performance goals. It is a much more complex cornucopia of choices, and many senior executives do not know how to develop a set of team goals that is distinct from, yet consistent with, their individual and overall corporate goals. As a result, the goal-setting picture becomes increasingly vague, less compelling, and more difficult relative to team performance. Teams at the top have a more difficult time establishing their performance goals than teams at the front line because

■ Their goals invariably overlap both corporate and line-of-business goals.

■ They also overlap the personal goals of individual executives.

■ The measures are often less clear cut or tangible.

Complementary Skills Give Way to Position

The extra performance capability that a real team provides comes largely from its complementary skill mix. Otherwise, any combination of individual efforts would do the job. In the mill or plant self-directed work team context, the right skill mix comes about naturally. Team members are selected primarily on the basis of the set of skills they will bring to the group. To do otherwise would seem foolish, even to those who do not understand the discipline of teams. After all, the purpose and collective task of the self-directed work team is based on an optimal meshing of the skill sets of several people.

As we learned from Mike Corey about Champion's Quinnesec mill, there are usually eight to ten people working the paper machine: a machine manager, a machine supervisor, a process engineer, a maintenance person, and about five to six people working the wet end (where the pulp goes in) and the dry end (where the paper comes out). Before, everyone focused only on their specific assignment or job. Now the team members are multiskilled, each understanding and able to perform more than one job on the machines and in other parts of the mill. Although their primary skill determines their position on the team, they can and do work in other positions to expedite performance and help one another solve problems quickly.

As team opportunities rise to the top of the company, the appropriate skill sets are not necessarily the most natural or obvious choice in team situations. Nor is it as appropriate for members to acquire skills from one another. Once again, the situation is a bit "grayer." For one thing, the team opportunities are much more diverse, and the skills required cover a much wider range. Often, a required skill set for a particular team opportunity does not exist within the formal senior leadership group. Although any group of senior executives can provide diverse skills among them, their roles in groups or teams are usually more a function of their formal positions than of their specific work or functional skills. Hence, team opportunities at the top are often staffed with executives who do not possess the right sets of skills for the situation at hand. It's one thing to presume that the senior leadership group will possess the right skills for a strategy-shaping project, but quite another to expect to find the right skills for a purchasing and materials effort.

There is no substitute for ensuring the right skill mix in any real team effort. It is true that each team member will develop his or her skills during the effort, but the base of competence must be adequate to permit that development. This skill-fit requirement is much more obvious at the front line than it seems to be at the top, where each executive is *presumed to possess all the skills required for any issue* the group may choose to confront. The converse is also true: all members of a senior leadership group feel a need to be involved in every issue, even though some members of the group can contribute little of value to particular issues. In sum, teams at the top have a more difficult time ensuring the right match-up between member skills and team tasks because

- The performance challenges are more complex and amorphous.
- The senior leadership group is presumed to have the skills for any issue it chooses to pursue.

▪ The representational and position attributes of senior executives are more likely to determine team roles than their individual working skills.

The Working Approach
Must Accommodate Part-Timers

The working approach that a potential team follows is a major determinant in how effectively the individual skills of its members are brought to bear on the group's collective work products. Each team needs to shape an individual working approach that takes account of the different skills and roles of the members. The members must become as committed to their working approach as they are to the purpose and goals of the team. The mill teams at Champion worked hard to shape working approaches that would capitalize on their skills and that were explicitly tailored to fit the membership. As we saw in the earlier examples, because front-line teams work together over extended periods of time, it is more natural for them to tailor the team approach to better fit both the skills and the working patterns of all the members.

It took only a few months for the senior leadership group at Champion to shape its current working approach—but it had the benefit of the previous two years of working together on the transition process. Like most senior leadership groups, Champion had in the past periodically established task force efforts at the top to deal with particular issues. Most of the time, however, these functioned as working groups, with a senior executive always in charge. Chapter 3 describes how major unexpected events, such as mergers, create real team efforts, but these are the exception rather than the rule.

As difficult as front-line working approaches are at the mills, they are not as challenging as shaping team working approaches at the top, for three reasons:

▪ The mill teams consist primarily of full-time members, whereas most top teams are made up of "part-timers" (members who can devote only part of their time to the team assignment).

▪ Top teams are usually determined by organizational position, whereas mill teams are based largely on working skill sets.

■ Working approaches at mill levels, once determined, tend to last longer, whereas team efforts at the top require constantly changing the working approach to fit different issues, problems, and priorities.

Mutual Accountability Is More Threatening

One of the critical litmus tests for a real team is the existence of true mutual accountability. Best characterized by the phrase "we hold each other accountable," rather than "the boss holds us accountable," it reflects the higher degree of commitment among the members of a real team. Champion's mill teams rather easily developed strong norms of mutual accountability, once the purpose and goals were established. Although the front-line workers were used to deferring to the lead foremen and hierarchical department managers, the team-based systems replaced them in favor of people with team leader capabilities. Also, as mentioned earlier, the machine team members are compensated on objective measures of their joint performance.

By the time executives reach top management positions, they have acquired experience and knowledge that is not easily replaced. Unfortunately, they have also mastered an executive leadership discipline that is not conducive to team behaviors. One of the cardinal elements of successful executive leadership is the notion of individual accountability. To suggest adding a dimension of *mutual* accountability threatens the simplicity and security of individual control on which most senior executives depend. The senior leadership group at Champion was no different, despite the success of team efforts in the mills.

The notion of mutual accountability is more troublesome to senior executives than it is to teams down the line because

■ Executives believe that consequence management demands clear individual accountability, or they will lose control of performance.

■ Many executives have not had any recent experience with mutual accountability to which they can relate.

■ It is more difficult to determine mutual accountability because of the diverse multiple responsibilities most executives have.

NONTEAM BEHAVIOR IS MORE NATURAL AT THE TOP

As Sigler demonstrated at Champion, a single-leader unit works well at the top. It requires a pool of strong, individual leaders who know the relevant marketplace, who are disciplined about setting high standards of performance, and who have the benefit of a well-designed set of supporting systems and management processes for monitoring and assessing individual results. This is sometimes referred to as the concept of "consequence management"; it is based on well-known principles of individual accountability. When these conditions exist, real team efforts are discouraged and often unneeded. They not only match the hierarchical experience of most executives, but they conform more naturally to the time binds at the top, because such units reach their full effectiveness as a group faster than teams can.

Nonteams Fit the Power Structure

The single-leader mode of behavior fits the expectations of the established hierarchy and power structure that governs most organizations. A "power alley" exists that encompasses the specific individuals up and down the organization who have the most "clout" and organizational jurisdiction, who make the critical decisions, and who are expected to align the decisions and actions of others with respect to corporate priorities. Single-leader working groups and organizational units fit within this model much better than real teams, because of their leadership clarity and individual accountability. Even though teams can be found in these situations, they invariably occur at random rather than by design. And, when they occur, the "establishment" or formal organization usually sees them more as communication or morale-building forums rather than as true performance units.

Nonteam behavior protects the natural order of things in the hierarchy, and strong leaders use that order to their advantage. They do not subscribe to rampant disruptions or widespread empowerment groupings as the best way to change a corporate culture. Nonteam behavior persists at the top simply because top executives prefer to function as individual leaders most of the time. They excel in settings where they can focus on achieving their individual best results, as well as hold others similarly accountable. They are natural overachievers as individuals; they are uncomfortable collaborators in amorphous groupings with overlapping accountabilities.

Early in their careers, top executives master the art of working within an orderly hierarchy. They become comfortable and effective using the power, predictability, and alignment efficiency that nonteam or single-leader structures preserve. Job responsibilities are clearly spelled out, lines of communication are well defined, and behavior patterns conform to established norms. Each executive knows what he or she is accountable for and to whom he or she is accountable. The lines of power and political influence are also clear and reliable; you know what to expect, whom to expect it from, and how to react in response. If someone isn't up to the job, he or she gets replaced by someone who is. That is what we normally infer when we hear that an organization needs a "tough-minded decision maker" at the top.

An orderly hierarchy not only protects the politics of power and pecking orders, it also protects the individual egos and comfortable patterns of experienced executives who have worked long and hard to get where they are in the organization. They know how to use the order to get things done without much fuss and bother. Each executive is part of a set of informal networks that respect the politics and structure of the organization. At the same time, these networks permit the special information and work flows that top executives require in order to be effective and deliver the results expected of them. Teams may be part of these networks, but the top executives play sponsoring roles (they commission, monitor, and support team efforts) rather than work as active team members or team leaders. It is a much more effective use of their time.

Nonteams Are Fast and Efficient

There is little question that the time factor at the top is a major element in the equation for determining the optimal balance between team and single-leader performance efforts. Not only is the single-leader unit a more comfortable mode of behavior at the top, such units also conserve executive time compared to real teams, at least during the initial phase of shaping goals and working approaches.

I first realized the importance of the time factor when two former colleagues, Ken Kurtzman and David Murphy, were reviewing the results of some research they were pursuing on management approaches in venture capital firms. They were seeking to understand more about the pace of change in those firms, because it is invariably much faster than the pace of change in other kinds of organizations. I was initially frustrated with our discussion, because Kurtzman and Murphy kept insisting they were encountering virtually no real teams in the organizations they were exploring. Obviously, I thought, their research must be faulty, and I was pursuing the argument accordingly when the lightbulb went on in my head. Of course, I said to myself, most venture capital situations are under such tight, demanding time schedules—virtually a matter of life or death for them—that they can't wait for real teams to form. They may sacrifice on the long-term performance scale, but they think they make it up in the short term. Hence, they demonstrate little patience for potential teams to pursue the time-consuming "forming, norming, and storming" stuff that team efforts commonly require.

The single-leader unit or working group can be energized and aligned by its leader relatively quickly. A seasoned leader usually offers the advantage of knowing what the group's goals and basic working approach should be. Thus the group hits the ground running. It can rely on the experience and formal position of its leader to make individual assignments clearly and wisely, protect it from unfriendly outside elements, and keep the members on track. Most misunderstandings among members are readily resolved by the leader. The group is likely to make fewer mistakes, because of the leader's level of knowledge and experience relative to the task at hand—*as long as the leader really does "know what is best" in terms of goals and working approaches.*

In marked contrast, a real team is more energized by a common level of commitment among its members—rather than by its leader. That commitment includes the purpose, goals, and working approach of the team. In the beginning, of course, the team leader helps to energize his or her team members until they reach the common levels of commitment that can come only from working together over time. Sooner or later, however, a real team becomes self-motivating. Its members establish goals that compel them to meld individual skill sets into a joint working approach that captures the best from each. That working approach also ensures a shifting of the leadership role to fit different task and capability requirements. In other words, the actual leadership of the team shifts back and forth among the members. There is little doubt that a real team is a powerful unit for both performance and change. Because it is able to deliver both individual and collective work products, its performance results are greater than what the same individuals would produce in a nonteam mode of behavior. It is the collective work products, mutual accountability, and ability to shift the leadership role that create both higher performance capability and greater leadership capacity.

The real team mode of behavior is more demanding on its members, *and in the beginning it is less efficient.* The members inevitably go through difficult periods of adjustment to one another as they are learning and sharing different know-how, experience bases, and insights. As Hackman's work (cited in Chapter 1) shows, the capacity for learning is directly related to the amount of trust among team members.[2] Learning requires trust, and the trust promotes learning, but all this takes time. It also takes time for the members to work their way through the variety of unforeseeable mistakes and misunderstandings that they inevitably encounter. There is little doubt that a potential team will take more time than a single-leader group to reach full effectiveness as a performance unit. Nonetheless, a fully effective team will outperform a working group—provided there is a high potential value from collective work products and multiple leadership capacity.

Figure 2.1 summarizes and compares the several elements just discussed which account for these differences. Obviously, the differences can have tremendous significance at the top of large organizations, because of both the premium on executive time and the upside potential of real team performance. As a result, leadership groups that can learn to shift back and forth between working group and real team modes of behavior will avail themselves of higher performance results and more leadership capacity over time. This demands a much different mindset, however, as top executives are instinctively more comfortable with the orderliness and clarity of single-leader working groups.

It is important to note that the time efficiency advantages accrue to the single-leader working group *only* for the time it takes for the group to master the discipline of teams. From then on, the race belongs to the real team.

Fragmentation Precludes Collective Work

In many industries today, the emphasis is on disaggregating the overall structure into lots of small business units. The idea is to get decisions made faster and closer to the marketplace. As a result, most perform- ance issues are being addressed below the corporate level, making the pressure for real teaming at the top appear less severe. After all, large, multinational companies rarely surface a performance issue above the major line-of-business level, and global issues that cut across different lines of business are usually within the functional purview of highly talented staff executives. These kinds of issues may constitute team opportunities within a line of business, but not across them or at the corporate level. The challenge lies in identifying real work that

Figure 2.1
THE PERFORMANCE LOOK-ALIKES

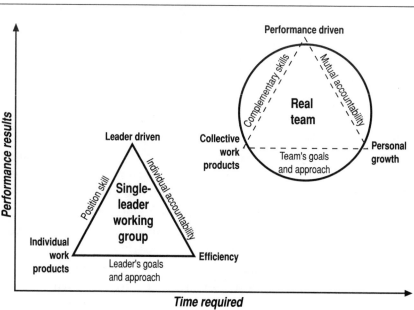

requires the collective skills of the senior leadership group. Hambrick's work sees this fragmentation among a CEO's direct reports as one of the most difficult problems in forging a cohesive group.

> The problem of nobody coming together around the table in the first place . . . the fragmented TMT, represents an enigma. The individual executives may possess all the information and energies to do their own jobs and mount their own parochial responses to the environment; but they are unable to engage in the internal exchange, collaboration, and mutual adjustments required to formulate company wide action.[3]

In other words, they do little collective work. This increasing movement of decisions closer and closer to the marketplace exacerbates the difficulty of identifying collective work for the senior group by shifting many of the more natural team opportunities away from the top level. This shifting of opportunities down the line, however, is creating a new mix of team opportunities at the top. Many of these are not yet as clearly recognized as the ones they are replacing, because they lie outside of normal lines of business and require a mindset that focuses on cross- and multibusiness situations. Most top executives are still much more comfortable focusing on the performance needs within their primary line of business. Thus senior leadership groups are more likely to attack such issues in an individual, functional, or working group mode—even when the situation offers high potential for a real team effort.

A collective work product is defined here as *the tangible result of several members of a group applying their different skills to produce a performance improvement not achievable by any one member alone.* More simply stated, it is the result of what two or more team members work on together. Because it is easier to define than to identify, a major portion of Chapter 5 is devoted to illustrating different types of potential collective work products at the top (strategic issue resolution, organization structure change, core process redesigns, people development), as well as describing the conditions required for such products to result in real team levels of performance. Collective work products are very important in shaping team composition, because they determine the skill mix that a potential team must have. Consider the following example from General Electric's (GE's) Motors and Industrial Systems business in Ft. Wayne, Indiana.

Jim Rogers, CEO of GE's Motors and Industrial Systems, is one of the better top executives I know when it comes to team performance. When he took over the electrical motors business at GE, it quickly vaulted from near-breakeven performance to over 20 percent return on its invested capital. He is one of the few CEOs I know who has successfully established "leaderless" real teams to run important business units, as well as product development, cross-functional, and front-line worker teams. Most of those groups that should function as real teams do so whenever the performance circumstances warrant.

One of my early encounters with Rogers came when he invited me to speak to a gathering of his worldwide middle and upper management group in Ft. Wayne, Indiana. After my talk, we discussed his 14-person potential team at the top; Jim was convinced he could shape them into a more effective real team. Over the next few weeks, we explored alternative ways to identify and attack real team issues. Each time, we had to admit that our issues did not require the full leadership group working together. We did, however, identify a number of promising subteam opportunities. A good example was Rogers' desire to accelerate the company's entry into India, clearly a high-priority opportunity of great interest to all members of the leadership group. It was not, however, something that all of them could contribute to, either individually or collectively. Nor was it something that was best explored without the talent of people outside the immediate top leadership group of 14. Two years later, while researching another topic with Rogers, I asked him how his team efforts within the top group were shaping up. He replied, "Some work, some don't. More often than not, we function best as a working group or in subteams—it's tough to find collective work for the entire group."

Rogers recognizes that real team performance requires collective work products that offer high performance potential. Even in an environment as advanced in the application of team basics as GE Motors, however, it turns out to be very difficult to identify suitable collective work for the entire senior leadership group. I believe this is true regardless of whether you are in the intensely competitive commodity motors business, a high-technology growth business, or a global financial services business. Thus neither General Electric, Hewlett-

Packard, nor Citicorp is yet run by a real team at the top—and that is not necessarily bad!

Unlike *The Spirit of Haida Gwaii* image described in the Introduction, you cannot simply force all executive creatures into a single boat, call them a team at the top, and expect to obtain real team levels of performance. However, you might well obtain a valuable consistency in their vision, strategy, and corporate performance aspirations. You could certainly expect to get them all pulling in the same direction within their individual roles and responsibilities, and you could expect them to make collective decisions reflecting common corporate aspirations and enforcing common performance standards. These are all worthwhile results. Nonetheless, the all-or-nothing notion (i.e., the group is either always a team—or it is not ever a team) finds few collective work products that will yield real team levels of performance.

The Popular Fallacy: "All My Direct Reports"

Many executives believe that team performance at the top of large corporations today is far less than the opportunity warrants. The research for the book *Wisdom of Teams* clearly supports that belief; Douglas Smith and I searched in vain for real team examples within the executive suites of large companies. Other than those rare instances of very personal, two-man teams like William Hewlett and David Packard, we came across very few, if any. Since writing that book, however, I have encountered literally dozens of senior executive groups that want to increase their team performance capability, because they believe they are missing a source of significant capacity to lead change as well as to increase performance. For the most part, they have not been able to capture that opportunity by simply relying on their instinctive sense of when and how to function as a real team.

The most limiting aspect of forced top team configurations—in other words "all my direct reports"—is the difficulty of shaping collective work of high value that fits the skill mix of the group. Such a task is analogous to searching after the fact for a market to fit an internally designed product, rather than first identifying the market need and then designing the product to fit. The same problem can occur with forced team configurations below the top, but there one usually finds more flexibility in adjusting the group composition to fit the task (or vice versa). Top executives are chosen because their individual capabilities and experiences qualify them for a very demanding responsibility. Team challenges at the top seldom require the particular mix of skills represented by the CEO's direct reports. Nor do such challenges often represent a clear priority over the formal and demanding responsibilities of the individual executives. In other words, it is hard to find collective work products that warrant all of the senior direct reports doing real work together—particularly if, as Hambrick was quoted earlier, you cannot even get them to "come together around the table."[4]

The instinctive approach to teaming at the top will remain disappointing as long as senior leaders hold to the "all direct reports" assumption about team composition. When a senior group is thus constrained, it seldom finds appropriate opportunities to which it can apply team discipline. The right mix of skills and the common level of commitment rarely match up with the performance task at hand. This difficulty persists even at some of the better-performing companies cited in this book, such as Hewlett-Packard and Citicorp.

HEWLETT-PACKARD'S WORKING GROUP AT THE TOP

Before Lew Platt became CEO of Hewlett-Packard (HP), he was an executive in the company's Medical Equipment Division. In that role, he was a member of one of the better organization and business unit leadership teams at Hewlett-Packard. Many of the business units in decentralized companies with strong performance ethics, like HP and GE, have leadership groups down the line that frequently function as teams. The flexibility of a real team leading a business unit provides an important advantage in responding to today's tough, fast-moving, intensely competitive markets. The Medical Equipment Division case was one such leadership group we explored for *Wisdom of Teams.* The group often functioned as a real team at the top of that business unit. When Platt moved up to a corporate executive responsibility under John Young, however, he joined a top group that functioned more as a working group than as a team. Although it worked as a team now and then, it was typically not the entire group of Young's direct reports, nor did it work as a team nearly as often as when Platt was on the Medical Equipment Division leadership team.[5]

Now that Platt is CEO, he still leads the company in what is basically a working group structure at the top. His direct reports constitute a small group of line and staff executives whose efforts are heavily consumed in leading and working their own areas of the business. Because of HP's strongly independent and decentralized management culture, there are few critical performance issues and opportunities that are not within the jurisdiction of one of the down-the-line unit managers or staff leaders. Hence, the corporate leadership group seldom feels a need nor has an opportunity to function as a real team on matters critical to performance results.

CITICORP'S PROJECT DELTA

Before Walter Wriston turned the CEO role at Citicorp over to John Reed, he created a classic, visible horse race for the top job. The obvious candidates were his three direct reports: Hans Angemueller, John Reed, and Thomas Theobald, each of whom represented different attractive combinations of strengths and weaknesses for the CEO role of the world's largest money-center bank of its time. Wriston employed a number of organizational shifts and special assignments while he and the board were considering the succession issue. One of the more perplexing of these was called Project Delta; it was a potential top team effort that never materialized.

The project, focused on corporate overhead costs, was initially delegated to the three heirs apparent. Theobald recalls that it was never really thought of as a team, nor was any single individual clearly in charge—a perfect recipe for confusion. Nonetheless, a number of special projects, task forces, and consultant-assisted analyses comprised this complicated attack on everybody's favorite scapegoat—corporate overhead cost. It should have been an easy target, but the confusing leadership roles made it more than elusive. The idea behind having a three-person nonteam was to make sure that the logical future leaders of the enterprise (regardless of which one became CEO) focused on the issue of corporate center costs. As Theobald viewed it, this was simply one of those "details" that Wriston did not want himself, so he assigned it to "everybody below." The fact that the three potential successors would be in an awkward and visible position of working together without a clear idea of who was responsible for what was simply not considered relevant.

Part of the problem was that everyone sensed that Wriston and his board were only weeks away from announcing a CEO succession choice that had doubtless been decided already. Hence, none of the three felt he was in a position to accept individual accountability, nor could he simply allow one of the others to be in charge, nor could they come together as a team. It was a classic catch-22 (no answer was workable) until Reed was anointed and could clearly spearhead the effort. As Theobald reminds us, "somebody has to be in charge at some point" if you want anything to happen—team or nonteam.

Wriston probably never expected the group to drive as a team to a joint resolution of the issue. Nonetheless, I believe it was *an instinctive reaction on his part to assign it to all of his primary direct reports.* Perhaps it was one last way of getting the three candidates exposed more broadly to corporatewide issues before making his choice known. Whatever his purpose, however, the group was a pseudoteam, with no chance of achieving real team levels of performance. It had neither the right mix of skills nor the common level of commitment to performance purpose, much less a common working approach. Confusing and frustrating as this may have been, it was not necessarily a "bad decision" if you factor in political intent.

When the CEO choice was announced a few months into the project, the situation resolved itself quickly, simply because the confusion over leadership and accountability disappeared. In fact, the project eventually achieved significant cost savings and was instrumental in Reed's initial restructuring of the company. Clearly, these were important accomplishments—but they could occur only after Reed, as CEO, replaced the three-person nonteam and put a single leader in charge. Would a real team effort at the outset have been significantly better? It is hard to tell, even in retrospect, because working groups accomplish many things as well as teams do.

CONCLUSION:
WE PRESUME INDIVIDUAL LEADERSHIP

To those not personally privy to executive suite pageantry, it may come as a surprise to learn that top executives cannot always behave as they might prefer. The people all around them—above, below, and beside—have sets of expectations for executive behaviors which are difficult to ignore. For example, most people expect their CEO to visibly "take charge," particularly in difficult, urgent, or performance-threatening situations. The hierarchy requires the CEO to make the corporate-level decisions. People become very uneasy and restless when they perceive any hesitancy or reluctance on the part of the CEO or any of his direct reports, to do so.

Boards of directors are particularly insistent on this point. They have only one practical way to maintain their fiduciary responsibility: hold the CEO singularly responsible. The primary act of control that a board can make is to replace the CEO when corporate performance falters; seldom does a board reduce the CEO's compensation or even fail to pay out large bonuses. Hence, it is critical for boards to be in a position to blame or credit the CEO, and many are literally terrified of concepts of mutual accountability and shared leadership.

You have only to read the latest issue of your favorite business publication to find examples of the similar views among most analysts and journalists on this question. They invariably attribute any significant corporate failure or success directly to the CEO, who, in turn, will likely point a finger at some individually responsible executive. "It happened on his watch" is a common phrase in business journalism when looking to explain significant performance shortfalls. Andrew Sigler, CEO of Champion International (Chapter 1), was a favorite whipping boy of the business press for well over five years, while he stubbornly pursued his high-risk strategy of heavy investment in big paper machines and "unproven" team-based mill management systems. When the company's financial performance seemingly vindicated Sigler's strategy, of course, he got most of the credit. Nonetheless, he seldom tried to explain his team leadership philosophy and approach to any of his board members, largely because he had learned the hard way that it was highly likely that they would "just not get it."

The 1996 change in the top leadership at Apple was a classic example of how the employees, the business press, and most knowledgeable observers look to strong leadership at the top for the answer. Steve Jobs was taken to task for his early overemphasis on overly creative new ideas, and John Scully for his overreliance on group consensus down the line. Gilbert Amelio was expected to put things right again, but given little chance of success by many in the press. And yet, all published coverage of this situation describes Amelio's changes with clear emphasis on the importance of "shaping his new team at the top." *The world at large wants to label every leadership group a "team at the top," but it really does* not *want it to behave as a real team.* That is perceived as much too risky.

The same expectations persist internally as well. Most top leadership groups, who may lament the absence of real team behavior, are actually much more comfortable in the single-leader working group mode. It lets them off the hook for team performance shortfalls, because they can simply blame the leader for their nonteam behaviors. This dilemma sometimes leads top organizational unit teams to consider team-building sessions to help create more open and constructive teamlike interactions. Top executives in high-performing organizations, however, have little time and almost no patience for team-building exercises. They instinctively recognize that teams will require more of their time than their current comfortable and efficient single-leader mode of interaction. They have incredibly demanding schedules in leading their own parts of the enterprise, and they have a hard time envisioning a high value added from trying to become more of a real team at the top. And, although others in the organization often complain about the lack of team behavior at the top, they can be even more critical of team-building nonsense. They expect prompt, decisive action from their senior leaders—as do we all.

CHAPTER THREE

How "Major Events" Spawn Teams

IT IS CLEAR THAT the forces at work on senior leadership groups favor nonteam behavior. We admire strong leadership at the top, and we expect top leaders to demonstrate decisiveness and wisdom in interactions with those around them. This is why even superior team executives like Lew Platt at Hewlett-Packard and Jim Rogers at General Electric have found improving the balance of team results to be more difficult within their senior leadership groups than elsewhere in their organizations. It is also why major, unexpected events take on a special significance in determining when, why, and how senior groups function in a team mode of behavior.

The typical pattern of behavior in top leadership groups in all kinds of enterprises is familiar and well established:

- The CEO designates his or her direct reports as a kind of executive council, ranging in size from 6 to 25, which includes the senior executives responsible for major lines of business and functional corporate departments.

- Their primary purpose is to shape strategic priorities, enforce operating standards, establish corporate policy, and develop management talent; they set the direction, mission, and policies for the enterprise.

- They meet weekly to discuss operating matters; many also periodically set aside extended time to discuss major strategic and policy matters.

▪ The CEO chairs the meetings, controls the agenda, and syndicates decisions among the members; agendas are circulated in advance, allowing only modest amounts of time for subjects not on the agenda.

▪ *The group functions primarily as an efficient, effective single-leader working group;* it occasionally spawns subgroups and single-leader task forces to deal with key issues, problems, and opportunities—but seldom applies the discipline of team basics to either the full group or the subgroups.

This pattern works well, particularly when the executives are experienced in their areas of primary responsibility and share mutual respect for one another's judgment and leadership capability. Occasionally team efforts occur, but for the most part only when unexpected issues and opportunities arise. And those issues must be sufficiently compelling to generate behaviors outside the normal organizational unit (single-leader-group) norms—which is much less often than one might hope. As a result, real team efforts at the top are largely driven by major events.

But this is no surprise. We are certainly not describing a new set of interactions at the top of most institutions. For literally centuries, the familiar pattern summarized above has guided governments, educational institutions, and religious orders, as well as business enterprises of all types and sizes. History provides ample illustrations of major events that have precipitated teamlike behaviors at the top for brief periods of time. For all we know, the forming of the United Nations, the Yalta peace conference, and even the recent work by the European Monetary Commission may actually have spawned unlikely team combinations—but if they did, rest assured that it was only for brief periods, on very pressing issues.

Major unexpected events have been opening up real team opportunities at the top for generations—and the natural instincts of good leaders have taken advantage of some of them. Moreover, reliance on this "instinctive teaming at the top" has proven effective in several strong institutions. The problem comes with the increasing pace and intensity of social, competitive, and technological change. Such change is creating two relatively new conditions with respect to the behavior of senior leaders within their so-called team at the top: a need for alternative modes of leadership behavior and the value of more conscious targeted application of the elements of team discipline (as summarized in Appendix B).

1. *Alternative modes of leadership behavior.* An executive's "personal favorite" leadership approach is increasingly unlikely to adequately address the broadening sources of strain on the enterprise. The pressures of competition are now joined by comparable pressures from governments, labor groups, and social factors to produce a higher-level—and more balanced mix—of performance aspirations. No longer is it enough simply to satisfy shareholders; customers, employees, suppliers, and the body politic are becoming equally prominent in the performance equation. As a result, senior leadership groups are learning to apply multiple leadership approaches with better balance and more rigor than ever before. *They simply need more leadership capacity to handle the diversity and pace of marketplace change.*

2. *Conscious targeted application of team discipline.* Many executives already recognize the value of a more conscious and rigorous application of the discipline required for real team performance in an increasing number of situations. Senior leadership groups who seek to optimize their performance contribution can no longer afford to rely solely on their natural instincts to signal the need for team behaviors. As this chapter will illustrate, it takes a major event to bring those instincts into play at the top of well-established hierarchies. As a result, *it happens all too rarely, and it tends to occur much too randomly; thus significant team opportunities are overlooked.*

It is a desire to preserve the natural order within their formal organization that makes most top leaders overly dependent on big events to open up opportunities for real team behavior. Once such events have run their course, the leadership group invariably returns to their more natural order: the efficient and comfortable working group. Consequently, major events take on disproportionate significance in determining when and how leadership groups at the top function as teams. Such events come in a variety of packages, but three in particular illustrate why and how an event that breaks up the natural order of top organizational unit interactions can create real team opportunities: major mergers and acquisitions, a major refinancing, and the advent of a new leader. In each case, real team opportunities at the top become more apparent, although not always more realizable.

MERGERS AND ACQUISITIONS

The opportunity to acquire or merge with another company invariably creates a number of real team opportunities at the top of both organizations—even when the merger or acquisition doesn't materialize. Any major merger causes top management to think about teaming at all levels. Special task forces are established to responsibly meld the best practices of the merging companies. Potential teams from both sides come together to exchange information, eliminate duplication, and develop integrated approaches at many levels. Some function as real teams; others do not. The SmithKline Beecham merger of equals illustrates this phenomenon particularly well.

Premerger Preparations

When Robert Bauman of the Beecham Group in the United Kingdom and Henry Wendt of SmithKline Beckman in the United States agreed to a merger of their two companies, they made history in more ways than one. The recent book that describes this unique merger in excellent detail points out how it was:

. . . the first of what later became a string of consolidations in the pharmaceuticals industry in the 1990s;
. . . the first to deliberately come together around a vision of "integrated healthcare";
. . . at the time, the largest transatlantic equity swap in business history;
. . . [and] one of the few transactions to be promoted and, more important, actually executed as a true "merger of equals."[1]

From a "team at the top" perspective, there is also little question that this major event created a series of significant team opportunities among the top leadership groups of the two companies. To begin with, the preparations and negotiations prior to the merger spawned several real team efforts among the top executives. For example, Bauman had already established a leadership approach at the Beecham Group based on an Executive Management Committee (EMC), which had worked in a team mode to shape the vision and strategy that led them to SmithKline Beckman in the first place. In fact, Bauman believed that "the first step had to be for the EMC to unite as a team working on *Beecham's* goals, rather than as separate business heads focused on their individual responsibilities."[2]

Once the two CEOs had agreed in principle to the merger, however, it was critical to build a case for change and a vision for the combined entity which both organizations could support. One of the team opportunities that this created occurred in mid-November 1988, when "about twenty senior operating managers from the two firms began several weeks of [working in] seclusion in a Manhattan lawyer's basement office . . . their output was to be the first business plan of the new company."[3]

Postmerger Management Challenges

Once the deal was completed, the major work of implementation began. Not surprisingly, Bauman formed a subset of the EMC later known as the Merger Management Committee (MMC). It comprised the key managers who would not only lead the integration of the two companies, but also literally shape the future of the combined company. Their role became "to provide guidance, philosophy, strategy, receive recommendations, and make decisions—but not to do it all. "[4] To make a long and fascinating story unfairly short, this led to literally dozens of real team opportunities at the top, involving a large number of top executives in different subteam situations. "Mergers create a built-in crisis that provides management with a unique opportunity: employees are waiting and expecting change to happen. Rather than allowing things to slow down, management must maintain the momentum and capitalize on the opportunity to make change happen."[5]

And one of the best ways to take advantage of that situation is to be rigorous and disciplined about identifying and cultivating team opportunities at the top. Most mergers will appoint some kind of merger management group, loosely labeled "team," but few of them are rigorous about applying the discipline that would yield team performance. Bauman and his merger team were better than most in this regard, which allowed them to carry off one of the most unique mergers and major performance transformations in modern corporate history.

Mergers and acquisitions are big, special events for most companies, so it has become fairly normal for merging companies to consider temporary joint teams at the top as well as down the line during the early stages of the implementation process. The conditions in merger and acquisition situations that lead to team performance at the top, though perhaps obvious, are worth summarizing briefly.

- A compelling sense of urgency readily apparent to people throughout both institutions

- New performance improvement imperatives (many that are measurable)

- Critical cross-company issues not resolvable without integrating the different skill sets of both organizations

- Overlapping formal structures and processes that require new informal networks for integration

- Merger (temporary) leader roles that differ from formal (permanent) leader roles

Thus it is natural for the senior leadership groups at the top of two merging companies to shift into team modes of behavior to complement their normal single-leader working group approach, both during the negotiating process as well as in the integration of the two organizations. People expect that behavior at the top and are generally comfortable with it. Other major events, less conspicuous than mergers, can produce similar conditions leading to team opportunities that are not always as visible to others. The next case describes a less-visible "big event" example from Browning-Ferris, a world leader in the rapidly expanding waste management industry. Note, however, the similarities of urgency, unique skill-mix needs, and temporary new leadership roles. These are all typical of events that create team opportunity at the top.

A MAJOR REFINANCING

In doing research for *Real Change Leaders*,[6] we became familiar with the enviable record of growth and success of Browning-Ferris Industries (BFI), the second-largest waste disposal corporation in the world. From a neighborhood garbage pickup outfit in 1969, the company's growth has been strong, except for one modest downturn in the late 1980s. For much of that period, the company has been under the dual leadership of William Ruckelshaus and Bruce Ranck, operating in tandem as CEO and COO. In 1995 Ranck became CEO. Although both men worked extremely well together, they divided their responsibilities so that the company has always been led at the top as an organizational unit team or single-leader working group. The senior leadership group includes top staff executives, as well as the four heads of the major regional operating units.

In early 1995, however, a major refinancing in the form of a several-hundred-million-dollar investment security product created an unexpected team opportunity at the top. The product was a unique, one-of-a-kind debt-equity offering called ACES (the acronym for Automatic Common Exchange Securities), specifically designed to accommodate the company's strong growth prospects. The waste management industry worldwide offers a wealth of opportunity for companies with the position and skills to exploit it. However, BFI would have been unable to fully exploit that opportunity without a major new injection of capital.

As attractive as the company's prospects appeared to be, a financing of this magnitude was not a trivial undertaking, and the potential downside of an offering shortfall was significant. Working diligently with their investment advisors, the top four executives (Ruckelshaus; Ranck; Jeff Curtis, the chief financial officer; and Ron Long, the treasurer) increasingly found themselves in a real team mode which occasionally included other executives as well. It easily met the three critical litmus tests of a real team:

1. Clear *collective work products* dependent on the joint application of multiperson skills

2. *Shifting leadership roles* to be filled by different people at different stages of the effort

3. *Mutual (as well as individual) accountability* for the group's overall results

The senior executives not only had to work together on the details of the offering, they also had to shape a dramatic but fact-based global "road show" that would convince potential investors worldwide to buy the new investment instrument at an attractive price. This meant several weeks of preparation in addition to several more weeks of intensive world travel. It was a global event that required meeting with potential investor groups and existing major stockholders, as well as conducting countless interviews with the business press. The financing effort took place in three phases: (1) the creation of the new instrument, (2) the approval process, and (3) the road show to market it.

Phase 1: The Creation of ACES

A major acquisition in the fourth quarter of 1995 brought the issue to a head. BFI would need some new financing just to meet the acquisition commitments. The ratings agencies, of course, expected BFI to use equity financing. However, top management's growth aspirations led them to seek a more creative instrument, which would be more efficient in terms of financing costs yet still provide the funding flexibility required to accommodate rapid future growth.

Although the creation process was led by Jeff Curtis, working closely with Ron Long and the legal department, the leadership of the group shifted back and forth among the members to match the particular issue at hand (finance, tax, legal) at different points in the process. They actually used two competing investment banks to work with the internal team to ensure the best possible instrument.

The result was a collective work product called ACES, which BFI believes to be the first of its kind. The instrument gives ownership of Treasury notes with a purchase commitment for BFI stock. For its three-year life, it is treated as debt financing (making the debt interest tax-deductible), although the rating agencies consider it the same as an equity. Thus it meets their equity requirements, while saving BFI roughly $25 million in net present value on a total financing of over $400 million.

Needless to say, the creation of this new instrument demanded multiple inputs, perspectives, and ideas from inside as well as outside the company. Ranck, Ruckelshaus, and Greg Muldoon (senior vice president of business development) were all heavily involved in the effort, because they had to understand the instrument in all its complexities. In addition, they needed to ensure that its risk and financial attributes would meet the company's overall strategic as well as financial needs. It was a real team effort—and ACES is an excellent example of a "collective work product" at the top.

Phase 2: The Approval Process

During an approval process that required several weeks of work, the same group was involved, again as a hands-on working team. Whereas, in the first phase, Ranck, Ruckelshaus, and Muldoon had been primarily in a listening, questioning, and advising mode, they took a more active role in the second phase. They knew it would be extremely important for each of them to develop a strong understanding of and a common commitment to the new instrument. Otherwise, they could have real difficulty convincing the board and other members of management, not to mention the potential outside investors.

The relative size and importance of the financing, as well as the different risk factors associated with the new instrument, made it mandatory that all communications by the senior team be very clear and consistent. Everyone needed to know it was a "big deal" that had to work. Although Jeff Curtis was responsible for the first formal presentation to the board of directors, other members of the top team were actively involved in preparing for that presentation, answering questions, and participating in discussions both before and after the formal presentation. Again, they were functioning as a real team, this time with Curtis rather than with Ruckelshaus or Ranck playing the leader role. It is a particularly good illustration of how senior teams can and do shift the leader role based on the task at hand—even though both the CEO and the COO were part of the team.

Phase 3: The Road Show

In the third phase, which lasted about a month, Ranck and Muldoon were the leaders of the two teams that went across the country talking to retail and institutional investors. During this period, the financial and legal management team took more of a back seat, although it was still involved in helping with presentations and questions. Other staff executives also played essential roles in shaping several elements of the road show. Because Ranck, Ruckelshaus, and Muldoon had been so intimately involved in the work of creating the instrument and obtaining the board's approval, they were extremely effective in marketing this very complex product to the outside world.

The elements of BFI's major financing event that produced real team results throughout all three phases are important to note.

- The obvious importance of the event to BFI's aspirations gave it an urgency that drew top executives out of their normal organizational patterns; instinctively, they worked together to apply their expertise in whatever way made sense in accomplishing their purpose and goals.
- The offering was sufficiently important to the success of BFI that hierarchy became much less important than expertise and coordination of very complex disciplines (such as treasury, tax, legal, and equity markets).
- ACES was a clear, compelling work product that required the collective action of several top executives working in multiple team modes.
- The groupings were small because of the confidential nature of the effort, but essential skills were obtained beyond the circle of "direct reports" from both inside and outside the organization.
- The working leadership of the group shifted back and forth according to the phase of the effort and the specific tasks within each phase.
- The team aspects of the effort were really not visible to very many people, either inside or outside the company, because of the importance of maintaining confidentiality.

While some aspects of the effort were carried out by individuals and by small groups working in single-leader modes, much of the work produced team behaviors and discipline. The ACES instrument was too complex to explain through normal communication channels, and the common level of understanding and conviction that was required prompted real team interactions. Once the offering was successfully subscribed to, however, the group members returned to business as usual within their normal organizational units. Nonetheless, they had achieved real team levels of performance that were of tremendous value (millions of dollars) to the company.

Major events like mergers, acquisitions, and refinancings have inherent advantages of breaking the normal patterns of leadership and introducing outside factors that favor teams. The same can be true when there is a change in leadership at the top—although this event does not always favor teams. When a new leader (the CEO) comes onto the scene, this is by definition a major event—often unexpected. New leaders create both positive and negative expectations throughout the institution, but particularly at the top. Many new CEOs revise the membership and roles of the senior leadership group—including replacing some, if not all. They will change job content, titles, senior forums, management processes, and people. There is no doubt that this breaks normal leadership behavior patterns and can thereby clear the way for team performance—provided the right leadership attitudes are in place (i.e., a belief in the potential performance value of teams).

Even the most individualistic of new top leaders unconsciously create team opportunity, although they seldom capitalize on it. The following story illustrates how a new leader materially influenced the balance of team and nonteam performance without fully recognizing the difference. Although the overall result wasn't necessarily bad, the effort did not exploit the full potential of the senior leadership group. The names are disguised to respect people's sensitivities without weakening the accuracy of the story.

A NEW LEADER SHAPES HIS TOP TEAM

"Winston needs to exert his leadership more often . . . (CEOs) can't afford to be so concerned about whether people will like it or not," said Dave Hart with a force and conviction consistent with his 20 years of Green Beret discipline. Hart is currently vice president of operations for Best Fuel Distribution Corporation (BFD).* His comments refer to Winston Newberry, CEO of this recent, highly success-

*Disguised example.

ful public offering of Fuelco. The comment was made in the context of Hart's generally positive overall view of BFD's future opportunity—" . . . provided we strengthen the alignment and discipline within our leadership group."

This is a surprisingly common complaint in companies where a new CEO is striving to build his own team at the top and create an environment where a mix of new and old executive leaders can learn to work more cohesively. In such situations, a CEO who attempts to step back and encourage other executives to step forward and work as a "team" will be viewed by many as not exerting enough leadership. On the other hand, when that same CEO steps into a strong leader's territory, the uninvited intervention is resented. It becomes a no-win game. There is little question, however, that the introduction of a new leader constitutes a major event that opens up new team and nonteam opportunities at the top.

In the spring of 1993, BFD, then a subsidiary of Fuelco, was no longer viewed by that company's leaders as one of their core businesses. Fuelco is a diversified energy company with a strong record of growth and profitability. At that time, BFD's profits were nil, although its revenues accounted for a large portion of overall Fuelco volume. From Fuelco's point of view, therefore, a public offering of BFD would significantly improve Fuelco's gross margins. Whereas BFD's operating profit potential was in the realm of rounding errors for Fuelco, it looked like a hidden opportunity to Winston Newberry and William Danford, who decided to buy a controlling interest in BFD. They could not help but believe that there must be an attractive "profit pony" hiding somewhere under BFD's nearly $5 billion in breakeven revenues.

Situation Summary

Apparently, according to Newberry, once they got rid of a few obvious misfit businesses, there were lots of hidden "profit ponies" to be found, with attractive upside potential. Although perhaps too soon to declare victory, the early turnaround results offer impressive support for his claim. The 1996 financials not only exceeded an already ambitious plan, but also posted the best year ever for the company, with a cash flow return on equity of well over 30 percent. This was clearly a remarkable performance compared with earlier years, and one that led the newly emerging senior leadership group to explore modifications in its overall leadership approach which would allow it to capitalize more fully on core capabilities and attractive future growth opportunities. The group members weren't too sure they wanted to be a team, however.

BFD is a crude oil–gathering business that buys, sells, and transports different kinds of oil products to and from various locations. Over 80 percent of its cost base is accounted for by trucks, pipelines, drivers, and pipeline personnel. It is a fairly complicated business that must negotiate and broker literally thousands of oil leasing deals among hundreds of customers every month. Its profitability is heavily dependent on an unpredictable and volatile market. In fact, although 1996 was a very good year, a decline in crack spreads (the difference between the price of crude oil before and after it is refined) in the refinery environment created an insurmountable profit problem in 1995.

The business is driven by trading and by maintaining good relationships with producers. Several factors appear to be important for success, namely (1) timely information on the differences between markets (which depends on good communication between different traders); (2) fast response to customer inquiries; (3) high accuracy in deal settlement; (4) taking appropriate risk positions; and (5) maintenance of customer relationships (which can easily be hurt by mistakes in operations, accounting, and finance). The pivotal functions are trading, marketing, scheduling, and operations (pipeline and trucking). Overall profitability is also affected by the portfolio of products traded, and BFD has done some acquisitions and outside hiring to broaden that portfolio.

Within this business and organization context, Newberry's newly emerging senior leadership group faces important challenges in developing the leadership capacity that will be required throughout the organization to continue its early turnaround performance.

The Views of Senior Leaders Differ

Not surprisingly, BFD executives refer to almost everything that involves more than one person as a "team." In reality, their ad hoc teamwork lacks common focus and discipline, there are few real teams, and there are even some problems in managing effective single-leader working groups. Although most executives acknowledge an urgent need for more teamwork or coordination at the deal level near the front line, they fail to recognize the causes that originate within the leadership group. Nor is there a common view of what changes are needed.

Each executive expressed a different view of what modifications were most important in the team at the top. For example, Newberry seeks a broader consensus among the group. He sees the real priority as a lack of teamwork and collaboration down the line. "We have to get middle managers working across their functional boundaries to help each other more in the interests of total BFD performance. We need a clear consensus among the top group to bring this about."

In marked contrast, Dave Hart sees a need for stronger leadership by the CEO. "People who can't meet expectations need to be dealt with sooner rather than later . . . we are all in this boat together," he said, "and if someone isn't willing or able to pull his oar with the others, the CEO has to deal with it." Clearly, Hart fears that Newberry's efforts at building consensus work against that end.

Ted Everett sees the issue strategically as well as economically. As a former consultant, he believes that a small group at the top must develop a compelling scenario that aligns how individuals attack the basic value drivers for the business. "Managers in each function need to understand much better than they do the impact that they each have on the bottom line for the total business."

Mary Pickett, the head of human relations, believes that the top group must learn to work and communicate more cohesively as a team. Mary is an astute observer of executive behavior. She knows what she is talking about when she says that the top executives are currently perceived by the rest of the organization as "not together" on many key issues. When they interact with their own parts of the organization, they often appear to be out of synch with points of view they reached as a senior leadership group. In addition, she worries about the apparent "two tiers" within the senior leadership group; that is, Winston and Ted often appear to be making key decisions without involving other executives who have relevant knowledge.

In short, the team opportunity for the senior leadership group of BFD depends a great deal on whose eyes are looking at it. In some ways, it is analogous to the classic Aesop fable about six blind men who felt their way around an elephant and came up with six very different descriptions of what an elephant is really like. What the situation appears to be depends on what parts of it you bump into. Nonetheless, the new senior leadership group of BFD had lots of real team opportunity, if they chose to pursue it as such.

How the Group Actually Functions

When we integrate an outsider's observations with the different executives' own views of the "elephant," a more realistic composite picture emerges. Newberry is an intelligent, analytic leader who prefers to establish a set of high aspirations, clear strategies, and fact-based parameters within which others can lead. His overall style is largely nonconfrontational, if not team-friendly. Unfortunately, what he intends as "providing head room" for others is often viewed as abdicating expected CEO responsibilities. Like most senior leadership groups, this one is a bit uncomfortable without strong and visible decisions and actions by the CEO from time to time.

Newberry's efforts to work with different pairings and combinations (which he tends to think of as teams) within his leadership group are sometimes viewed by others as creating a special "tier" within the group—or even as intentionally excluding others from critical discussions. His style of asking penetrating questions is sometimes viewed as not understanding the business, or simply probing to get people to "do it his way." Mary Pickett describes an initial frustration she had in working with Winston: "Everything I said, it seemed, would lead him to punch something into his calculator. I finally had to ask him to put the calculator down, or tell me what he was calculating so I could understand how he thinks about the business."

The few "natural team acts" that manage to survive are nourished by very compelling performance challenges, such as an acquisition. When an unexpected or uncertain opportunity of high potential appears, the right executives will group around it and occasionally function in a real team mode. Major decisions, however, are invariably individual or single-leader events. The group actually does work well in subgroups or teams on specific problems or opportunities. But, without a conscious effort to differentiate and apply the appropriate discipline, the results are far less than the potential. Acquisitions are easily the most obvious team challenges, because various executives will group and regroup among themselves and with others outside the core group at key points in the acquisition process. Many of these groupings are short-lived, but they are real team efforts nonetheless. Because they constitute natural team situations, the senior leaders have little trouble functioning in a team mode.

Time becomes the enemy of more extended team efforts, particularly on urgent, unexpected issues. The need to meet tight personal and group agendas precludes open-ended collective work, and shifting the leadership role seldom takes place in any potential team situation. Ad hoc groupings often exclude leaders who could contribute and who do not fully understand the reasons for their exclusion.

Occasionally, a different kind of issue will result in a formal small-group assignment (rather than an ad hoc grouping). For example, the systems issue is being addressed by a group that consists of Mary Pickett, Ted Everett, Dave Hart, and one or two others with relevant skills. This particular group often functions in a real team mode. Again, the importance of the issue, the collective work needs that require different skills and perspectives, and the cross-functional scope of the issue make this a natural team situation. The group functions in that mode comfortably, but much too often without the kind of discipline that would ensure real team levels of performance.

The senior leadership group is not perceived by themselves or others to be unified or consistent in philosophy and priorities. Areas of general agreement within the group are not consistently conveyed throughout the organization, and the critical priorities are often misunderstood. What most people, particularly those outside the core group, can observe of the group's interaction is often only partially accurate. Hence, natural small group interactions can be misread as special tiers or exclusionary groupings.

The Paradoxical Role of the CEO

Unless the CEO takes charge of certain visible aspects of the situation, real team behaviors suffer—and CEO credibility suffers as well. Leaders at all levels expect more decisiveness and direction from the top— from both the CEO and the senior leadership group. Paradoxically, they expect more teamlike behavior within the group as well. It is extremely difficult for any CEO to play a team leader role unless he or she also steps up to the strong, nonteam decisions that the group expects of him or her.

This is particularly true for a new CEO, whose constituents still do not know exactly what to expect. It is not so much a matter of personal style as it is a matter of both recognizing the different roles people expect and being able to help others understand those situations where the *unexpected* role may, in fact, be the better role for the leader to play. Striking an appropriate balance between strong leadership direction and real team effort is a difficult, moving target. The challenge is to be able to play different roles at different times, consistent with the kind of issue or opportunity at hand. Chapter 7 is devoted to a full exploration of the different roles for leaders of top executive groups.

MAJOR EVENTS ARE NOT ENOUGH

The good news, of course, is that major events sometimes create team opportunities that lead to real team performance at the top. The bad news is that simply waiting for unexpected big events to trigger team behavior can seldom optimize the balance between teams and nonteams at the top. Such random team efforts by senior leadership groups fall well short of both the potential and the need. Obviously, the pressure for a better-balanced senior leadership approach has its roots in the marketplace forces of speed, complexity, and change—but these do not always precipitate major events. In fact, when such forces create a major event, it is usually because a leadership group has not recognized the early signs of marketplace change and therefore has to make a major catch-up adjustment.

The conscious, disciplined pursuit of team performance to complement, not replace, executive leadership performance should not depend on major events. This logic helps explain why an increasing number of CEOs are actively searching for ways to obtain better balance of individual and collective performance from their senior leadership group. Their search reflects two important beliefs:

1. What works with real teams below will also work at the top.
2. Real team efforts can expand leadership capacity at the top.

These beliefs deserve further explanation, because they are not as obvious or widely shared as they might appear.

Teams Below Are Showing the Way

Many of the external pressures for real teams at the top have been around for a while. The new pressure is from the groups below, members of which are becoming change leaders in their own right—particularly in their wisdom about teams. They are showing the way for those senior leadership groups that are paying close attention. The workplaces of companies across the economic spectrum are making use of team performance (without making the mistake of pursuing a "team-based organization"). Self-directed work teams, product design teams, sales account teams, cross-function expert teams, process redesign teams—you name it, and you are likely to find it in more than one kind of business. Unfortunately, this team know-how and experience rises too slowly on its own within the typical corporate hierarchy.

More important than this team proliferation, however, is the increasing focus on the basic elements of the discipline that ensures team performance. A few years ago, the corporate world was being victimized by a different set of so-called teams, including involvement, empowerment, sensitivity, and even teamwork teams. The focus on performance had been temporarily lost, and in many companies, it still is. This situation is the primary reason why a number of top executives have developed strongly skeptical views of the team movement. The "team-based organization" became a dangerous idea, if not a dirty word, in the minds of those who saw it lead to the pursuit of instant teams everywhere. And they were right!

Today, however, the notion of performance is central to the various team efforts in well-managed enterprises. This performance focus, however, is easier to obtain the closer the unit is to its marketplace, because customers and competitors energize natural team instincts and discipline in the workforce more readily than any other source. As you move up the leadership ladder, it is easy to lose the sharp concentration on collective results in the marketplace that differentiates the real team from potential or pseudoteams.

Mobil's current team efforts at the top of the company have their roots in team actions down the line. One of the most notable was the formation of asset management teams in the U.S. Exploration and Production operations in the early 1990s. These started out as leader-driven units with a close-to-the-market profit responsibility as the hallmark of their approach. The motivating force for many was simply "beating the competition." Because of Mobil's decentralized philosophy, each of the asset management teams developed somewhat differently. Some of them functioned regularly in a real team mode; some, as working groups; and some, as organizational unit teams. In fact, the effectiveness of the units often masked to the casual observer the difference between those that functioned primarily as single-leader working groups and those that had become more real-teamlike in their leadership approach.

Either way, these collective leadership units made a major difference in Mobil's way of thinking about management and leadership up the line. Other groups around the globe in marketing, refining, and chemicals were undergoing similar experiences. In each case, the transference of team skills seemed to get sidetracked at the upper management levels, particularly within the new Fairfax, Virginia, headquarters complex. Top management approaches stayed cleanly within the organizational unit leader philosophy, sometimes even holding onto outdated vestiges of command and control. Remember, this is the oil industry, where command and control have long been the philosophies of choice. Gradually, however, the pressure for a different leadership notion was wedging its way into Fairfax. Several top executives found it difficult to ignore the downline team performance that they were experiencing. And, although it took several years for these notions to reach the Executive Office, they eventually made it.

So it is with company after company. Team behaviors below produce extra performance results, as well as extra levels of satisfaction and energy, throughout the workforce. Seeing these results, upper-level managers and executives begin the application of similar discipline at higher and higher levels. Sooner or later, the senior group in an increasing number of companies is, like Mobil's Executive Office, forced to confront the fact that it is missing the kind of team performance that is commonplace in several other parts of the company. And, as real team performance below mounts up, leaders at the top find the pressure harder and harder to resist.

In Pursuit of Leadership Capacity

The notion of "leadership capacity" is extremely important here. It is not simply a function of the number or quality of individuals in formal leadership roles. Rather, it implies a system of leadership, if you will, that can extract leadership wisdom, insight, and behaviors from many more individuals. Thus it fuels the continuing search for different kinds of leadership approaches, both individual and joint, at all levels of the organization. In fact, many downsizing, restructuring, and reengineering efforts are actually reducing the number of leadership and management positions in the formal structure. The objective function of all this is *to expand the capacity for leadership and independent initiative without having to increase the number of individuals in formal leadership roles.*

One of the largest enterprises in the world recently came to a startling conclusion after a major reengineering and downsizing of its corporate center; namely, that its first line of leadership below the senior group had only a dozen or so qualified, proven candidates for senior management roles anywhere in the world—and the CEO honestly felt that he could express full confidence in only a handful of those. This was at a time when the senior group was but a few short years from retirement. This company is not alone in facing a talent shortage with respect to its next generation of leaders. The pressure on such senior groups becomes even more severe when they are constrained in their ability to work easily in different leadership configurations and modes of behavior.

Few successful enterprises today believe they have enough leadership capacity to capitalize on their marketplace opportunities. Top executives in all sectors of the economy lament the shortage of everything from "good general managers" and "professional staff specialists" to "real change leaders" at all levels. This lack of leadership capacity eventually tracks to the top leadership group. Yet few executives recognize how and why real teams actually expand leadership capacity within a top leadership group.

Team configurations, when they work, actually extract more relevant leadership contributions from the same number of individuals— even at the top of a large organization. The self-directed business unit leadership teams at General Electric were cited earlier. These provide a good illustration of how leadership capacity is extended at the top of companies or units run by leadership teams. When I first learned of these units at GE's Motors and Industrial Systems business, I expressed modest surprise. I shared the concerns that most executives would have with a notion of no clearly designated general manager who could be held accountable for profit unit performance. In fact, I inadvertently blurted out something like "You can't do that with a team, Jim!" Rogers (CEO of GE Motors) replied, "Well, we're already doing it." As I explored further how these units worked, it became clearer to me why the risk of not designating a general manager for each of his several business units was a wise one for Rogers to take.

In the first place, this is a company and a business that truly understands the discipline of team performance and how to obtain it. Thus, when Rogers established a team to run one of his business units, they were rigorous about applying the basic discipline of team performance. In other words, they got the skill mix right, established clear-cut performance goals, shaped a working approach that took full advantage of their skill mix, and set out how team members would hold themselves jointly accountable for business performance.

Just as important to the skeptics, however, was what I'll call Rogers' "escape hatch." If for some reason, after a reasonable trial run, one of his business unit leadership teams was not performing, Rogers could—and did—simply appoint someone to take charge and shift to a single-leader working group mode. All that was lost in the process were the few months of floundering by the dysfunctional team before designating a leader. Since most of these units do, in fact, prove able to function very well in a team mode, the risk is well worth taking. But then Rogers knows what he's doing when it comes to teams.

The gain in leadership capacity in this kind of situation comes from two obvious, but often overlooked, sources. First, you obtain the needed general management contributions from several less-than-fully-developed leaders. The collective unit will invariably contain four or five people of different leadership profiles, as well as different skill and experience profiles. The team mode creates a strong leadership unit with a balanced mix of somewhat "flat-sided" leaders. Their leadership development in one or more areas is not yet complete enough for them to function in a full general manager role—but as part of a balanced "general management team," they can function extremely effectively.

Second, leadership capacity is increased because the formal organization now requires one less general manager in each unit. That role is filled by the collective group, whose members are also individually filling key functional or market-based management roles. In effect, this eliminates a layer across the business units; namely, the general manager layer. It is not, however, an approach to be tried by those unwilling or unable to rigorously apply the discipline of team basics.

This same kind of capacity extension occurred at Mobil when a major change in the structure of the operating units eliminated the need for three full-time senior executive roles responsible for major lines of business. When Lucio Noto (Mobil CEO) refocused his three senior line-of-business leaders away from their traditional roles, he immediately began crafting a variety of new ways to use them in resolving critical corporate strategic and global positioning issues. After a year of working with this new configuration, Noto commented, "It's really great to have [this kind of senior talent] available for some of these unexpected critical global opportunities . . . it simplifies my life a great deal." Leadership capacity at that level, however, can be very difficult to come by without taking full advantage of critical teaming opportunities.

CONCLUSION: MAJOR EVENTS— A PARTIAL ANSWER AT BEST

As significant as major events are in opening up team opportunities, they are by no means the obvious answer to creating lasting team capability and performance at the top. In fact, they are but one of the reasons causing more top leaders to pursue a better-balanced leadership approach. Equally, if not more, pressing are the well-recognized forces of intensifying competition, increasingly diverse market segmentation, and exploding technological innovation. The multifaceted target and definition of corporate success demands more than a single-leader working group at the top that can convert to a team mode of behavior only when a crisis strikes. Nonetheless, there is a great deal to be learned from major event behaviors.

What is clearly needed is an integrated system of leadership and management—both at the top and throughout the enterprise—that can encompass and nourish both the informal and the formal elements for influencing organizational behavior *at the same time*. The either/or mindset in senior leadership groups is what makes them so dependent on major events to unleash team performance. It is also what causes some of them to avoid the single-leader groups and formal hierarchy in a misguided pursuit of a totally team-based organization. In both cases, they fixate on their favorite approach, and are determined to make it work in all situations; thus it takes a major event to break the pattern.

In their recent book, *Built to Last*, Jim Collins and Jerry Porras make a compelling argument against the "Tyranny of the OR" versus the "Genius of the AND." They point out how difficult it is for "the rational view to live with two seemingly contradictory forces or ideas [leadership approaches] at the same time. 'The Tyranny of the OR' pushes people to believe that things must be either A OR B, but not both."[7] Their research provides convincing evidence that truly visionary companies have become masters of "the AND." They appropriately quote F. Scott Fitzgerald, *"The test of a first-rate intelligence is the ability to hold two opposed ideas in the mind at the same time, and still retain the ability to function."*[8]

Similarly, the primary challenge facing senior leadership groups, who seek more team performance at the top, is to learn to accommodate both teams and nonteams at the same time—*with or without the benefit of major events*. If they persist as a single-leader working group that is dependent on major events to jar them into a team mode of behavior—or, conversely, if they insist on converting every group effort into a team approach—they will fall short of their potential to lead high-performing organizations.

Shortly before writing this book, I was fortunate to attend an informal luncheon with John Reed (Citicorp) and Lucio Noto (Mobil), two of the executives who generously agreed to let me share some of their top team experiences with readers. The purpose of their lunch was to share with each other their experiences, ideas, and efforts on the subject of accelerating the development of leadership capacity, both at the top of their corporations and down the line. What was most impressive about the lunch was how high a priority each of them placed on the resolution of this issue going forward—and how intent both of them were on finding ways to achieve a more balanced leadership approach at the top that could better integrate team and nonteam performance.

Neither was satisfied with his corporation's efforts thus far, although both could cite remarkable progress. Noto described his efforts to accelerate this development through a set of top-management councils, several of which were rapidly learning to function well in real team modes. Reed described his approach to building the capacity from the bottom by relying on a set of processes that his head of human resources had borrowed from a former employer, General Electric. Obviously, there are some top team actions implicit in those programs as well.

In each case, their focus on team performance at the top has increased significantly in the last few years, and they are working to achieve an even better balance. Performance is the objective function that both hold high, and expanded leadership capacity is the energy source they emphasize to that end. I believe both have abandoned the "Tyranny of OR" in thinking about their senior leadership groups. Their use of real teams at the top is only one piece of that puzzle, but it is one that has an increasingly high priority for them and for most other top executives in high-performing companies that I know.

CHAPTER FOUR

Two Disciplines That Conflict

My clearest memory of membership in a highly disciplined group was, not surprisingly, in the military. During the Korean War, I was enrolled in the U.S. Navy's Officer Candidate School in Newport, Rhode Island. The program was 16 weeks of nonstop pressure applied through a maniacal combination of mentally demanding educational activities with physically and emotionally demanding military training exercises. It was a combination only the Navy could conceive.

As with any artificially accelerated pressure situation, all kinds of unexpected reactions, behaviors, and disciplining occurred. For example, two of my section mates, Ed Dorsey and Joe Conway, were determined to beat the requirement for spit-shining their shoes, which normally took over two hours of concentrated hand-polishing. Because they had overheard a couple of the regular enlisted sailors assigned to the school describing how heat could make the polishing process go more easily and a lot faster, they decided to try it. Unfortunately, their cigarette lighter overheated the polish container, and it exploded—spraying black polish all over their room and themselves. The punishment for that little violation of dormitory decorum was the loss of two weekend passes for Dorsey and Conway—plus, of course, the 16 hours of sweat and elbow grease it took them to clean the polish splatterings off their walls, clothing, and faces.

Another of my section mates, Don Goetz, became literally paranoid about obeying the rules for guarding confidential information. One night during a late (1:00 A.M.) surprise inspection, as the rest of the company was assembling on the front drill field, we sighted Goetz struggling along the upper balcony walkway of our dormitory. Unbelievably, he was lugging a 200-pound footlocker on his back. It seems that Don couldn't remember the combination for the lock on his footlocker, and he was afraid to leave his "Confidential Study Guide" inside unguarded. The punishment for that midnight mental lapse was special latrine cleaning duty for a month.

Such incidents are laughable in retrospect, but at the time we believed they were dead-serious indications of what Navy discipline demanded of its future officers. A far more serious incident occurred when another of my classmates, John McBeth (disguised name), turned himself in for cheating. As he talked with his instructor after turning in a navigation quiz, McBeth became aware of a careless mistake he had made on the exam. When the quiz period ended, the instructor inadvertently left McBeth's paper behind. McBeth took advantage of that oversight to quickly correct one of his errors before returning the paper. After all, he had known better anyway, and it was only a weekly quiz. Less than an hour later, however, guilt got the better of him, and he returned to the instructor's office to confess. His punishment was dismissal from the OCS program, three years' mandatory duty as an enlisted man, and a general rather than an honorable discharge. This negative record followed him throughout his career, well beyond his naval service. Rigorous discipline can be like that; it leaves no margin for error.

Webster's defines discipline as *a set of rules or training that corrects, molds, or perfects*. Like the military, team discipline consists of a simple set of rules that must be rigorously adhered to if it is to result in the extra levels of performance that real teams can achieve, particularly at the top. Executive leadership discipline also consists of a simple set of rules, which is often in conflict with the rules teams must follow. And executive leadership (individual leader or nonteam) discipline needs to be equally rigorous if top executives are to achieve the levels of performance expected of them. The *basic conflict between these two disciplines poses the central issue* for senior leadership groups seeking to optimize their performance, and it is one of the major obstacles they face in their quest for a high-performance organization. This chapter addresses three important aspects of resolving this issue:

1. Recognizing that the conflict persists regardless of the environment.

2. Understanding the contrasts and recognizing the sources of conflict.

3. Seeking integration, rather than compromise or domination, of one set of rules over the other.

THE CONFLICT PERSISTS

While Ron Burns was a top executive at Enron, he worked on top-team challenges in very different environments: the pipelines and the financial services businesses. One of his favorite books is *Flight of the Buffalo* by James Belasco and Ralph Stayer.[1] He likes it because it captures a contrast that is at the heart of his distributed leadership philosophy. In the early days of the American West, buffalo herds thundered across the Nebraska plains where trains and automobiles now run. These herds were completely dependent on the head buffalo for every decision and action affecting their livelihood. Without their leader, the herd was in disarray. Burns recalls the book's contrasting analogy of a flock of geese that assemble and fly to their destination with no particular leader—many or all can and do lead as the terrain, weather, and wind conditions warrant.

Burns prefers a flock of geese to a herd of buffalo, but he also believes he must draw out *both* the individual *and* the team leadership capabilities of as many of his people as possible. At Enron, Burns pursued this balance within two different organizational environments—both more used to following a head buffalo in achieving attractive performance results.

The Pipeline Team Environment

When I first met Burns, he was president of the Enron Gas Pipeline Group. At the time, he was actually trying to change the culture of the pipeline group. Jeff Skilling, a past partner of mine who is now president of Enron, had invited me to attend a working session on the subject of culture change that Burns was leading with about 30 of his top people. At that time, Burns' perspectives on change were more advanced than mine, so I added little to the discussion. I did, however, learn a lot from the session, and I gained my first perspectives on Burns' ability to sense the mood and tenor of a group—and to shape its effectiveness without dominating its agenda or discussions.

He ran the session adeptly, but more as a working group than as a team. Partly because he had already launched several successful real team efforts within the company, he instinctively recognized that "changing the culture" of the company would not provide enough of a focused purpose for this large group to function as a team. That did not mean, however, that their contribution as a working group was trivial. Burns is a good example of a top executive whose team instincts allow him to recognize when a group can function in a team mode of behavior, as well as when it should not function as a team, and how each mode creates significant performance value in the appropriate situation.

Over the years, under Burns' and, later, Stan Horton's leadership, the pipelines developed team performance capabilities down the line as more and more of their workplace efforts converted to teams. It has been an uphill struggle, but much like Champion (Chapter 1), their teams down the line are making a difference. Neither Burns nor Horton, however, would claim to have run the business with a real team at the top. In fact, David Schafer, who now develops some of the best team efforts within Enron Gas Pipeline Group, argues that getting real teams to survive in the company's operations and marketing activities is tough enough. Obtaining team performance at the top will have to wait its turn.

Despite many efforts with teams down the line, Schafer believes the company is just beginning to develop a cadre of team leaders among middle- and upper-level managers. Only recently has management begun to understand the difference between real teams and single-leader units, and appropriately capitalize on both of them. Surprisingly, this is probably the most important distinction leaders at the top need to understand to achieve team performance at the top.

The Individual Performance Environment at ECTS

Following his tour leading the pipeline business, Burns joined the senior leadership that launched Enron Capital and Trade Services (ECTS). This group of diverse executive talents have literally transformed Enron from a regional natural gas pipeline company into an undisputed and widely envied leader in the energy field worldwide. Kenneth Lay, Richard Kinder, Jeff Skilling, Rebecca Mark, and a host of other uniquely individual talents produced remarkable results for Enron shareholders. To this day, Burns maintains that many of his most valuable individual leadership skills developed while working with and learning from these leaders.

> I feel like I played with the best when I was at Enron—and learned something about leadership from each of them. Kinder's instinctive ability to create a sense of urgency, Skilling's amazing capacity to focus on the issues that mattered, and Lay's genius for getting such a mixture of high talent people together in the first place . . . you can't work with that kind of talent and not benefit from it.

Basically, Burns is referring to many of the elements of the "executive leadership discipline" described in Chapter 1—he learned them well. He also learned that relying only on individual performers and single-leader units can complicate and frustrate the task of sustaining a high-performance environment. Collaborative, collective efforts can be valuable as well, even at the top. Although he found this hard to accomplish at ECTS, there is little doubt among those who worked with him that Burns contributed significantly to the success of several leadership group efforts, in both team and working group modes of behavior. Many times he was the glue that held such groups together—a role that few others played as well.

Most of the time Burns was at Enron, the senior leadership group functioned as individuals or in a working group mode that favored the individual skills of high-powered executives. To those "outside the room," they seldom appeared as a real team, although Ron recalls instances when they had to work in a near-team mode or pattern of behavior, even if only for short periods of time. And it often fell to him to find a way to bring them into working harmony and get their remarkable individual skills refocused for a short time on a critical collective work product.

One such example occurred when they were struggling with a back-office (sales and order processing operations) capability that had been rendered virtually obsolete by the rapid growth of their financing business. The demands placed on the back office were simply overwhelming relative to its capacity to process them, and the systems and service units that had been patched together to make do were taking days to process orders that should have been completed in hours.

Of course, every member of the "top team" had his or her own right answer to the problem. Everyone's answer had some validity, but they were neither consistent nor implementable. Working from behind the scenes, as he often did, Burns realized that there was no magic answer that would satisfy everyone. He therefore initiated a series of small, informal group sessions, punctuated with one-on-one discussions in between, that led the group to collectively design a multiple task-force review of the back office. This may sound simple enough, but without Burns' instinctive ability to bring these high-powered executives together as a team for brief periods of time, a viable solution would have been much less likely to emerge. Most people in the company, however, were completely unaware of these relatively brief team efforts.

To the casual observer, the only real team activity occurred down the line within special task forces or front-line workforce teams. Only those in the room at the time could have observed the top group shifting into a team mode. And it is unlikely that any members of the group recognized, or even thought about, the change in their mode of behavior. What some of them recognized, however, was the fact that Burns could enable the group to function more constructively as a group even though he was not at the top of the pecking order.

Behind Closed Doors

It isn't all that unusual among successful "teams at the top" for their real team efforts to be unobserved by others. It turns out that the best corporate leadership groups have been "secretly" shifting in and out of natural team modes without telling the rest of us—behind closed doors, so to speak. It may not happen often, *but it does happen!* And, in a great many cases, these shifts occur without the members realizing it themselves; it is mostly an instinctive reaction to unexpected events, as illustrated in Chapter 3. Others very seldom see it because the issues being addressed are usually urgent, sensitive, and confidential—and the time frames are short. Real team behavior requires a basic and simple discipline that can be applied by many executives, not an intricate set of interpersonal skills that only a few possess. Most good executives have worked in team modes at some points in their careers, although usually at lower levels. Like riding a bicycle, however, team skills aren't easily forgotten or difficult to revive. So, when a near-crisis situation demands it, top leaders will function as a team, even if behind closed doors.

Those who are guilty of doing it behind closed doors, however, probably pay a price in the missed opportunity to demonstrate visible, powerful role model behaviors that would motivate teams down the line. Because few people throughout the organization realize that the top executive group does periodically function as a team, "invisible team acts" do not catalyze or stimulate disciplined team efforts below. Nonetheless, it is naive not to recognize the team performance that does accrue behind closed doors on the executive floor of some of the better-managed companies in the world.

A Burning Desire for Team Performance

Burns' decision to leave Enron wasn't easy, and in the end, it came down to something "a lot more important to me than money." As his career progressed, he found that he savored the satisfactions of team leadership and performance beyond what he could obtain within Enron's stable of talented, high achievers, where individual performance was the critical factor for success and where the discipline of executive leadership prevailed. He says,

> I think a little like Tommy Lasorda [former manager of the Los Angeles Dodgers], who says he wants his team members playing for the name on the front of their jersey [the Dodgers] not the name on the back [their individual surnames]. I really get more satisfactions out of a team accomplishment than I do out of an individual one.

Although this desire for team satisfactions and performance at the top eventually led Burns to seek a more balanced leadership opportunity elsewhere, it was also the primary factor behind many of his team accomplishments at Enron. Nonetheless, he gradually became convinced that he was in too much of an individual performance environment to suit his aspirations—particularly at the top of the dynamic, high-performing Capital and Trade Services business. Populated by dozens of sharp financial analysts, traders, and investment bankers, it is a business that thrives on individual ambition and earning opportunity. It's hard to find real teams in that kind of fast-paced investment banking and trading environment—particularly at the top. The strong individual leader discipline is too much in conflict with the equally demanding discipline required for real team levels of performance. Table 4.1 compares the conflicting elements in the two disciplines.

Burns left Enron in pursuit of more team opportunity at the top. Much like Andrew Sigler at Champion, Burns remains a true believer in real teams, and both leaders had to confront a disturbing paradox:

Table 4.1
THE PRIMARY ELEMENTS OF CONFLICT

Single-Leader Discipline	Team Discipline	Elements of Apparent Conflict
Create and maintain urgency.	Create a meaningful purpose.	Meaningful purpose does not always equal urgency.
Resolve the critical issues.	Commit to team performance goals.	Specific goals of team not always "critical issues."
Enforce individual accountability (you win or lose on your own).	Mutually accountable (no member can fail; only the team fails).	Either/or mindsets fear a weakening of individual accountability.
Leverage executive time and talent.	All team members commit to real work.	A questionable use of top leader time.
One leader is decision maker for the group.	Team shifts decision role among the members.	Team decisions often not made by the leader.
Strive for the best individual talent.	Strive for the right skill mix.	Teams staffed against different criteria.
Periodically "raise the bar."	Members establish the height of the bar.	Teams lessen leader's power to raise the bar.

being a true believer does not make it any easier to obtain real team performance at the top.

UNDERSTANDING THE CONTRASTS

As mentioned earlier, the five basic elements of team discipline derive from a simple definition of a real team. In *Wisdom of Teams*,[2] we refer to those elements as "team basics," and they are summarized in Appendix B. Each element is as essential in achieving team levels of performance at the top as it is elsewhere in the organization. Unfortunately, team basics are more difficult to adhere to at the top, because they conflict with an equally demanding executive leadership or single-leader discipline. Too often, well-intentioned leaders fail to achieve the potential of team performance simply because they cannot adhere to team basics without departing from the single-leader discipline they hold dear.

All elements of team basics must be adhered to rigorously—like Navy discipline, there is no margin for error. One of my partners, Michael Murray, uses an analogy that emphasizes this point. Mike claims that the only way a student could earn "honors" at the Catholic Jesuit high school he attended was by achieving straight As in all courses. There was no margin even for an A- or a B+. A similar condition holds for team discipline: only groups that achieve the equivalent of an A on each element of team basics can expect real team levels of performance.

In 1996 the senior leadership group at Mobil went through a major reshaping of its top organization and leadership approach. It's a good example of how several strong executives wrestled with the need for more leadership capacity in the midst of a strong, single-leadership environment and potential team demands on their time—probably the most critical tradeoff between team and single-leader disciplines at the top.

In Pursuit of Leadership Capacity at Mobil

While the Executive Office at Mobil was in the midst of reshaping its corporate leadership role (described in Chapter 5), it encountered many of the common conflicts that top executive groups often face in functioning as a team. Perhaps the best examples occurred during the sessions the group had for the purpose of evaluating the performance record and development needs of the next-lower tier of leadership talent.

In the past, this task had been carried out as a normal part of a fairly typical human resource evaluation process. Forms were compiled, summary evaluations by superiors were obtained, and the top 75 to 100 executives were reviewed by the senior leadership group in a somewhat perfunctory set of discussions that focused mostly on personal impressions and judgments. As a result of Mobil's corporate center redesign effort, however, a number of critical reassignments were now required. Everyone felt a much greater degree of urgency about the top evaluation process.

In fact, this senior team effort had been preceded by a commendable team effort of the next level of executives. Their purpose was to accomplish a more rigorous and fact-based set of evaluations of potential candidates to fill the key roles in Mobil's new organization structure (described in more detail in Chapter 7). This group had essentially worked through a new process that became the model for the Executive Office's final assessment and position assignment process.

Members of the Executive Office (EO) were dedicated to this task because of its obvious importance to the company, but it presented them as top executives with a number of difficult tradeoffs. The most obvious difficulty was simply finding the additional time that would be required to complete a series of extensive evaluations that could not be delegated to anyone outside the EO itself. Members would need to conduct confidential interviews with several people, develop summaries of the findings, identify issues and questions for group discussion, and guide his or her colleagues through a group discussion of each person. This went well beyond the time the EO would have devoted in the normal human resource process. And it involved a lot of hard work.

The next task was equally difficult. The EO members were evaluating people who did not fall within their normal organizational purview or firsthand operating experience. They were used to making personal judgments on such people, but not in probing into their performance records and leadership experiences. Nor had they ever taken the opportunity to learn, from the bottom up, the "360-degree" evaluations (which provide managers with blind comments from those who work for them) recently adopted throughout the company. Like most successful top executives, they took pride in their ability to evaluate and judge potential leaders. The new process, however, required much more time and effort than simply relying on their past exposures. Moreover, these more intensive evaluations required very different behaviors from the top executives than their normal strategic, policy, and operating issue discussions and interactions. This was unfamiliar territory requiring uncomfortable behaviors. To some at first, the process seemed overly burdensome compared with the result: a set of fairly straightforward decisions on about 25 key positions. Was this really a wise use of that amount of top executive time? Obviously, the Mobil executives became convinced that it was, particularly because they saw the effort as entirely consistent with the primary focus of executive discipline: to better evaluate and reward individual performance, potential, and accountability.

Contrasts That Produce the Conflict

The question of "best use of executive time" characterizes the reaction that most top executive groups have when confronted with an unexpected team challenge. They are conditioned to a set of executive leadership rules that are well proven over time and that produce consistently good results in more time-efficient ways. Unfortunately, the commonly accepted code of executive behavior—discipline—does not include many of the basic elements required for team performance. Top executives are supposed to

- Direct and *lead the actions of large numbers of people*—whereas a team *molds the skills of a small number of people.*

- Exercise *personal judgment* in assessing risks, resources, and strategic options—whereas a team makes *collective judgments* through open dialog, conflict resolution, and real work.

- Make *assignments based largely on formal positions* in the formal organization—whereas teams members' *assignments are made on the basis of the specific required skills*, regardless of their formal organizational role.

- Be primarily *responsible for broad corporate strategy,* policy, and objectives—whereas a team's purpose and goals must be more tightly *focused on specific performance results.*

- Leverage their time and experience through *efficient organization and management processes*—whereas a team is *seldom the most efficient grouping or process* for getting something accomplished.

- Pinpoint *individual executives to make the critical decisions*—whereas a team makes critical decisions in a variety of different ways, using *whatever person or grouping will yield the best decision.*

- Manage performance of the organization by establishing clear-cut, *individual objectives and work products*—whereas a team must establish *joint objectives and deliver collective work products.*

- Be *individually accountable for "whatever happens on their watch"*—whereas a team must hold itself *mutually accountable for the collective results of all members.*

These contrasts produce conflicts that are difficult to resolve. The fundamental point, however, is that *both disciplines have their place in the senior leadership of any performance-oriented organization,* but it takes unusually perceptive executive judgment to determine which discipline fits different performance situations. The best executives struggle with this choice all the time; others may follow a less frustrating set of rules. Certainly, it is simpler to rely on the proven single-leadership discipline, except when matters of overriding team significance force the issue. The best leaders, however, make a conscious effort to apply both, recognizing that they will not always make the right call. Therein lies the challenge of top leadership.

INTEGRATING RATHER THAN COMPROMISING

"No one really wants to compromise, because that means a giving up of something . . . when two desires are *integrated,* . . . neither side has had to sacrifice anything."
—MARY PARKER FOLLETT

It was 70 years ago that Mary Parker Follett framed her seminal thinking about the concept of integration versus compromise in the world of organizational conflict. Those ideas, while lost from the corporate view for many years, have stood the test of time better than most. Her writings on this topic, encapsulated in the above quotation, are still relevant to the senior leadership challenge of integrating the discipline of executive leadership with the conflicting discipline of teams. As illustrated in earlier chapters, these two disciplines embody conflicting sets of ideas and desires about how to address performance challenges for a senior leadership group. Both have merit that can easily be lost unless the group works hard to find ways to balance the power and potential in both. Fortunately, the apparent conflict between the two approaches is seldom irreconcilable. Follett's thinking is helpful here, as Graham observes in her excellent synopsis of Follett's writings:[3]

> Her great insight was to recognize that conflict was not necessarily pathological or a manifestation of failure. It was, rather the "appearance of difference."[4] Difference was unavoidable in the world, and since it reflected a variety of opinions and interests it could be used creatively. Follett identified three "main ways" of dealing with conflict.
>
> (1) Domination by one party . . . offered a quick solution, but one that was unstable because it bred resentment and unconstructive because it suppressed nondominant perspectives that had the potential to add value.
>
> (2) Compromise, the second mode, was likely to leave all parties dissatisfied and to result in a suboptimum solution.
>
> (3) Integration, [which Follett advocated] . . . entailed a search for an innovative solution, "in which both [or all] desires have found a place."
>
> . . . She warned that it would be naive to assume that integration is always possible, but claimed, nevertheless, that it is often feasible and worth the attempt.[5]

Unfortunately, Follett's concept of integration is seldom nourished within the walls of organizations that depend on the reliability and efficiency of well-designed formal structures and management processes. These institutions count on that formal construct for the alignment of decisions and behaviors of people at all levels, but particularly at the top, where logic and order prevail.

Obviously, functional integration is what the best general managers and top leaders are supposed to provide as part of their ongoing individual leadership roles. To the extent such institutions obtain integration and alignment assistance from the informal or social construct of the organization, however, it is usually by chance. I believe the integration of team and executive disciplines requires more conscious attention, as well as trial and error, and give and take—plus plain old hard work—than formal structures and processes typically provide or accommodate at the top. Integration efforts can easily become a bit too disorderly and unpredictable for most executives.

Similarly, the informal construct of organizations (sometimes referred to as the social or cultural context), although certainly more receptive to the disorderliness of team behaviors, is actually less rigorous in applying team basics. In the formal organization, teams have to discipline themselves and fight the hierarchy to survive. Because the informal construct is less rigorous and clear, the survival of small groups of many other kinds is easier; hence, pseudoteams are much more common. Witness the proliferation, just a few short years ago, of "empowerment groups" (so-called teams) within large organizations. Because these efforts seldom produced real performance teams, top leaders quickly became disenchanted with them.

In both cases, the problem stems from either/or mindsets that are virtually oblivious to the important contrasts between a team and a single-leader group, and the very different advantages that each can offer. As a result, both are applied randomly (and therefore suboptimally) with respect to different performance opportunities. Those leaders who seek a true integration of the two disciplines need to recognize three realities about how each is viewed within the formal and informal contexts of organization:

1. The formal construct strongly favors the executive or single-leader discipline because of its time-efficiency and individual accountability.

2. The informal construct promotes undisciplined team efforts, because that construct sustains only a "secondary interest" in near-term performance.

3. Changing the mindsets within both constructs is essential to achieving a more balanced leadership approach.

Within the Formal Construct

Formal structures and processes are invariably designed to accommodate and enforce single-leader accountability. They presume *individual* accountability and are designed to pinpoint *individual* responsibility. Moreover, the preponderance of experience that top leaders have had during their careers has been in single-leader environments. They know the discipline works. They have relied on it successfully in hundreds of situations across dozens of years; it is second nature to them now. In contrast, their firsthand experience in applying the discipline of team performance is much less extensive and often less current. Although they see teams performing throughout their organizations, that observation cannot have nearly the impact of a hands-on experience. And, because they are experiencing executive leadership discipline every week, they have much more confidence in that discipline. Teams appear more risky to them.

When in doubt, the single-leader discipline usually represents the best risk/reward option. If you have a leader with the experience and knowledge for the issue or problem at hand, it is natural to appoint him or her to be the leader and simply call the group a team. That's par for the executive team course. If the situation turns out to require a team after all, and the pressure for performance is strong enough, the group may shift into a team mode on its own. This is particularly likely to happen if members of the group understand the discipline of teams and the leader is receptive to that approach, as we saw with Champion in Chapter 1. And, if the situation turns out not to require a team, leading off with a single-leader approach will usually enable the group to reach a resolution in the most time-efficient way.

At the same time, the factor of risk triggers one of the stronger arguments for developing real team skills to supplement executive leadership skills at the top of the organization. The leadership group that becomes adept at shifting into different leadership modes to fit the risk/reward characteristics of a wide variety of situations is the group that will optimize its performance results over the long haul. Otherwise, it will consistently go with the low-risk, high-comfort alternative and thereby lower its upside potential. To expand a bit on the message of Chapter 3, the problem with relying only on major events to stir the natural team instincts among top leaders is that such events must be very compelling to overcome executives' natural reluctance to take on the heightened risks of a less-proven team approach.

Give a good executive a fresh, firsthand experience with team performance, however, and you will likely witness a battlefield conversion of some kind or other. It doesn't take much to rekindle old team instincts and skills, and most executives have experienced them at one time or another in their past. Gene Renna, a member of Mobil's Executive Office, is a good case in point. His early frustrations with his new Executive Office role stemmed in part from his long and successful executive performance record. He knew better than most how difficult and ambivalent a top executive's situation can become, and how important it is to make tough decisions based on a solid base of experience and judgment that takes years to accumulate.

When Lou Noto asked Renna to tackle the question of top organization restructuring, he took it on without a second thought because he had been a prime mover in getting Noto to address this issue. The challenge was to design a governance and organization approach to address four extremely challenging business and strategic issues: (1) the petroleum industry was undergoing a number of dramatic and significant trends, and the end-games in many lines of business were becoming increasingly uncertain; (2) Mobil's global position was strong but not yet fully capitalized on, and the risk profiles of most attractive investment opportunities were increasing; (3) some of the most experienced and capable executives in the company were nearing retirement; and (4) many of those who would inherit the challenge of running the company in a rapidly changing competitive environment appeared to lack the breadth of experience to match their talent.

Simply put, the company needed to find a way to accelerate the development of its next generation of leaders, while building on its global position in an increasingly uncertain and changing environment—all without sacrificing near-term profit performance. Not a simple task by any measure. Moreover, no single executive knew the answer to this dilemma, nor was it clear what combination of structure and management processes made the most sense. With time running short, it isn't surprising that Noto looked to Renna to solve the puzzle within the context of strong executive leadership discipline. Gene had a very strong record of developing top people and was intensely concerned about the situation already. Noto was used to having a single point of accountability and liked to know "whom to look to" for the results.

Nonetheless, it also is not surprising that Renna instinctively worked the problem more in a team mode that included other members of the Executive Office and an outsider. This initial core team expanded its composition over the course of the redesign work, to include the substantive contributions of Walt Piontek and Bob McCool, two highly capable and experienced executives who were *not* members of the Executive Office. Renna didn't really think much about the fact that he was putting together a real team, or that he was departing a bit from the single-leader discipline that he typically applied. In his mind, he was still the executive "on point" for the results of the effort. Yet he instinctively knew that some kind of team effort was the only way to get this difficult organizational design problem resolved and implemented. In that context, Renna functioned well as a real team leader. (Again, however, note how the importance of "the event" opened the door for team discipline.)

An important by-product of the effort was the reemergence of Renna's conviction about the team potential of the Executive Office in its new role. He wasn't yet ready to trade in his proven executive leadership discipline for team discipline, but his attitude toward the Executive Office team opportunity definitely improved. He still maintains, wisely so, that "there are times to use teams, and times *not* to use teams." His firsthand team leadership experience with Executive Office members was probably worth more than all the advisors, team books, and team-building exercises in the world in convincing him that the team opportunity could actually include Mobil's most senior leadership group.

Another example of the difficulty of tradeoffs between executive leadership and team discipline was the BFD example in Chapter 3. Recall that Dave Hart, the former Green Beret, really struggled with the paradox of CEO Newberry's supportive behavior in letting Hart run his own show and the strong need Hart felt for more tough decision making by the CEO. The integration of strong executive leadership discipline and rigorous team discipline will likely remain more of an art than a science.

Because formal organizations are designed, in both structure and process, to promote a clear focus on individual roles and responsibilities (i.e., individual accountability), they postulate the most efficient use of managerial time and talent. Top executives, particularly in high-performing organizations, become masters of the wise use of their time. Some rely on calendar control, some on executive assistant screening, and others on sheer intuition for what's worth the time and what isn't. There is scarcely a demand or a request placed before top executives that does not cause them to assess the time tradeoffs; it's something they end up doing in their sleep. One of my partners once advised a client executive, whose schedule was choking him, to consider scheduling his appointments in 15-minute increments instead of 30-minute or 1-hour increments. Whatever works!

Teams are swimming upstream in this executive river of time trade-offs. I must confess that I did not actually recognize the importance of the time factor until after writing *Wisdom of Teams*. In fact, Jim Rogers of GE can argue effectively that real teams are sometimes as fast as or faster than single-leader efforts—once they become real teams. Therein lies the difficulty, however; it normally takes longer to put the discipline of teams to work than it does to simply rely on the experience and know-how of a leader who knows what he or she is doing and can make the necessary decisions quickly.

Within the Informal Construct

The senior leadership groups of high-performing organizations no longer concern themselves only with the formal construct of structure and process. The informal or social construct of networks, ad hoc forums, and informal interactions often becomes the differentiating factor in change situations. Although the informal construct tends to favor small groups and flexible units, all too often it overlooks the importance of discipline within such units. Lacking the discipline, the units remain pseudoteams, potential teams short of their promise, or simply single-leader units. Nonetheless, even at suboptimal levels of flexible unit performance, the formal organization cannot function without the ad hoc forums and networks we usually think of as the "informal organization."

McKinsey is a good case in point. Clearly, the firm lays claim to a strong performance ethic and can cite over 50 years of superior results to support its claim. Its formal structure and management processes, while important—particularly in the people development areas—are not as important as the informal construct within a truly global arena. Literally dozens, perhaps hundreds, of informal groups and interactions take place annually across, around, and over McKinsey's formal structure and processes. These networks deal with client matters, knowledge development, people development, and external relations of all kinds. Some have been "designed in," as in the sectors that shepherd the firm's knowledge and expertise in particular industries. Many of them emerged informally, but there is now a design structure that helps to ensure their effective functioning on a worldwide basis.

Most of the networks, however, were not formally designed, but rather emerged in response to client needs, market developments, or the simple initiatives of individuals and groups across the firm. McKinsey could not function without these networks any more than it could function without its formal structure of offices, client service teams, and people management processes. The same holds true for most organizations, although few rely as heavily on the informal construct as does McKinsey.

Yet the majority of the interactions and forums in the firm's informal networks have designated single leaders who take responsibility for convening, scheduling, prioritizing, integrating, and disseminating for their groups. Sometimes we label such a leader as the "convenor," to encourage team behavior, but this seldom works. Occasionally a real team effort will emerge, but most of McKinsey's real teams occur within important client assignments where a natural urgency and complexity of problems requires it. And, even there, as described earlier, a strong component of single-leader work groups often prevails.

Obviously, teams are important options within both the formal and the informal constructs. The problem that teams have in the informal construct stems from the absence of apparent or priority performance pressure. The groups that comprise McKinsey's informal networks are seldom as motivated by performance pressures to adhere to team discipline as those within the formal client service structure. This isn't necessarily bad, but those of us who understand the discipline of teams, as well as the firm's informal construct, can argue strongly that many significant team opportunities are missed. Several years ago, for example, I was in charge of the firm's organization practice and attempted to shift the leadership of the group from a single-leader mode into a team mode. The attempt failed, largely because of the demands on the time of each potential team member. We simply were not disciplined about shaping a working approach that could sustain a team effort in the face of strong individual priorities from active and pressing client situations. Although it was difficult to argue at the time that the tradeoff between near-term client urgency and longer-term organizational knowledge building should not favor client urgency, it is also hard to look back and not argue that we missed a longer-term opportunity for the firm. Unfortunately, I must admit that we were guilty of dealing with the tradeoff in too much of an "either/or" mindset. We fundamentally needed the leadership capacity that would have allowed us to accommodate both.

Changing the Mindsets

Within either the formal or the informal context of an organization, the challenge for senior leadership groups is to break the prevailing "either/or" mindsets of leaders, which cause nonteams to prevail in situations that warrant a real team effort. This is far from easy, because both constructs support a set of basic beliefs that permit only random integration—again, occasionally prompted by "big events." The formal construct believes that performance results demand disciplined leaders in pursuit of demanding individual goals; the informal construct believes that its purpose is communication, interaction, and social benefits, rather than near-term performance. Neither set of beliefs, however, can stand alone against the test of sustained, balanced performance over time.

Changing these mindsets and basic beliefs to integrate team and nonteam efforts for more than a few random events requires hard work (as Follett's writings demonstrate). It also requires a better recognition of the options that senior leadership groups can pursue in terms of modes of behavior, membership configurations, and leadership roles. The following three chapters address these options, the tradeoffs they imply, and how different top leadership groups have learned to apply them.

CONCLUSION:
MORE THAN ONE DISCIPLINE COUNTS

The leadership of a high-performing enterprise certainly requires discipline. The best CEOs apply an executive leadership discipline that places a premium on individual accountability for profit and market results, speed, and growth. The business press demands it, Wall Street rewards it, and boards of directors expect it. Consequently, CEOs organize a senior group to take full advantage of the executive experience and business skills of their best leaders. They establish efficient top management processes and forums to bring those leaders together to share experiences, insights, and judgments in shaping overall enterprise strategy and policy. Each executive in the top leadership group is expected to deliver against tough performance standards in his area of responsibility. He or she is also expected to "wear the corporate hat" in any involvement he or she may have in corporate issues. In troubled or turnaround situations, this single-leader discipline is even more stringently applied. Any executive who cannot make tough decisions and meet demanding turnaround goals and time frames is replaced—often from the outside.

Teams have a difficult time surviving within this discipline, even though many executives have good team instincts and skills. Unfortunately, a real team requires a different kind of discipline to achieve its higher performance potential—and the application of that discipline requires additional executive time, which is a scarce commodity. Hence, it usually takes a major, unexpected event to break the executive leadership pattern enough to permit the natural team instincts of top executives to work. As a result, there are fewer team efforts at the top than are warranted in most organizations.

Over time, the persistent reliance on single-leader working group patterns can result in a senior leadership group that (1) loses its ability to identify important team performance opportunities at the top, and (2) becomes sloppy in applying basic team discipline. The more senior leaders rely on organizational unit teams and single-leader working groups, and the more they concentrate on the application of their executive leadership discipline, the less likely they will or can apply a team performance discipline when required.

There is little excuse for any top leadership group's not learning and maintaining its ability to apply the discipline of teams, as well as the discipline of executive leadership. How else can group members make a conscious tradeoff with respect to their options? If the only discipline that a would-be team at the top can use and be comfortable with is the executive leadership discipline, it cannot access team performance capability when it needs it. Team performance at the top demands the same disciplined attention to the elements of team basics that it requires anywhere else in the organization. Top leadership groups present special problems and pressures in the application of that discipline, but it is critical to have the option.

This is not to argue that team discipline should replace executive leadership discipline. It is important that both of these performance disciplines remain in good working order in the toolkit of any top executive group that intends to lead a high-performing organization. Again, Mary Parker Follett provided a useful capstone for this chapter many years ago, when she observed:

> I know chief executives who do not act as umpire and decide between their executives. They try to integrate the different points of view, for they know that if they take A's and reject B's, they will lose whatever advantage there might be in B's view. The clever [executive] wants to get the advantage of both A's and B's views and so he tries to secure such an interplay of their different experience and different knowledge as will bring them into a co-operating agreement.[6]

This same line of reasoning applies to top executives who wish to obtain the advantage of the different capabilities represented by both executive leadership discipline and real team discipline.

CHAPTER FIVE

Collective Action Opportunities

T EAM PERFORMANCE AT THE TOP is all about doing real work together. And real work is *not* the same thing as open discussion, debate, decision making, and delegation of authority. The authors of *From Promise to Performance* (referenced earlier) hit the nail on the head when they described the work involved at the top during the international merger between the U.S. pharmaceutical company SmithKline Beckman and the U.K. consumer products company the Beecham Group:

> The best way to achieve management alignment was to have the EMC [Executive Management Committee] *work on a task together.* The harder and more important the task, and the more integral its members felt the EMC was in accomplishing that task, the better the chances of them coming together.[1]

As discussed earlier (Chapter 3), *From Promise to Performance* describes a one-of-a-kind merger of equals and major culture-change effort that involved thousands of people between 1986 and 1993. It is one of the few complete and credible analyses on record of successful transformational change. The results cited in the book speak for themselves. The example was used earlier to illustrate how a major merger event opens up team opportunity. It also contains a number of good illustrations of the kind of collective work that characterizes senior leadership groups that obtain real team levels of performance.

I spent a few hours with Robert Bauman, recently retired CEO of SmithKline Beecham (SB), prior to his writing efforts, to learn his views on teams at the top. Bauman had been chairman and CEO of Avco, a $4 billion financial services and aerospace conglomerate, and vice chairman of Textron before he took over at Beecham to lead the major turnaround merger with SmithKline. I was particularly impressed with Bauman's grasp of how a senior leadership group relies on real work tasks in its struggle to integrate executive leadership and team disciplines. His book describes his determination to meet demanding performance goals while combining the very different cultures of a pharmaceutical business and a consumer products business into an integrated health care company. At the top, both the EMC (Executive Management Committee) and its subset MMC (Merger Management Committee) were often involved in collective work efforts, while Bauman was holding them to tough individual performance standards. For example:

1. ***Shaping a new strategy.*** This was the first collective work effort Bauman used to unite the group as a team working for Beecham's goals (referenced in Chapter 3). This was a full two years prior to the actual merger, but it was the essential first step in Bauman's relentless quest for a better-performing enterprise. Although they drew on the inputs of outside consultants, staff advisors, and downline managers, the real work of shaping the strategy was a collective effort within the EMC. It was "a good vehicle around which to build the team . . . [but] it had to be *their* strategy, and that could evolve only if they developed it together."[2]

2. ***Setting postmerger integration goals.*** Just as he had used meaningful strategy-shaping work to build commitment within the EMC, Bauman quickly focused the MMC on working out the answers to the tough postmerger questions: "in the end, what was their goal? . . . what were they trying to achieve through the merger?"[3]

3. ***Using simple, unifying themes.*** The importance of simple themes is evident throughout the effort. Although these themes had their origins in a particular idea or phrase, they were clearly worked through jointly by the EMC and the MMC. The phrase "Now We Are One" grew out of the simple imperative of having to work together across the different cultures at all levels, including the top. And, later, the main theme for their culture change—"Simply Better"—emerged from working that same territory.[4]

4. ***Working on key issues to build trust.*** Contrary to conventional wisdom, Bauman had to launch the change effort before he had the ideal or right team at the top to lead the new enterprise. "Speed was important. 'Change while you can' was one of the lessons they had learned through the integration process." Early on, Bauman took his group to a place called Chewton Glen on England's south coast, where they spent the better part of three days working together to develop the behaviors they must exhibit to help SB realize its strategy. To work as a team meant building trust. To that end, they focused on the resolution of one key issue that would carry SB into the future, and that was "something bigger than each individual's interest that they could work on together."[5] The early notion of "something bigger" eventually led them to frame a "Statement of Values" that became the basis for developing a new set of "Leadership Practices."

5. ***Establishing clear small-group priorities and work rules.*** It eventually came down to setting priorities as a group and being "more focused and consciously disciplined about their demands on employees." Step one was a simple, but critical one "to limit future EMC meeting agendas to ten items (compared with the present eighteen)."[6]

6. ***Shaping the rollout process.*** Having decided on "Simply Better" as the brand for their change effort, and having agreed on a "Statement of Values" and "Leadership Practices," the EMC tackled another challenging collective work product: designing a practical rollout process. "They now spent as much time working through exactly how they were going to get the organization to personally take on the culture as they had worked as a top team to own the Values and Leadership Practices."[7]

Collective work efforts like these that warrant the diversion of executives' time and talent from their formal positions are much more obvious at the top of companies undergoing major change. Moreover, not all collective work products constitute a real team opportunity, for collective work can be leader-directed if the leadership role does not need to shift.

The reason collective work of significance can be elusive at the top lies in the relative importance of each executive's primary responsibility, which obviously deserves a very high priority call on his or her time. As a result, top leadership groups go to considerable lengths to make their collective time as efficient as possible. They do not seek out collective work products for the sake of having something to do together. At the same time, they can easily overlook high-potential performance opportunities for the company because their mindset is on leveraging their time rather than on working together.

The SmithKline Beecham story is about much more than teams at the top or collective work. Nonetheless, it provides convincing illustrations of how important real work is in integrating a strong executive performance discipline with the often conflicting discipline of teams. At the heart of this integration challenge are three key issues addressed in the rest of this chapter:

1. What constitutes a collective work product opportunity at the top?
2. Why do unifying themes and initiatives help energize and focus the group?
3. How does a leadership group maintain collective momentum over time?

WHAT IS A COLLECTIVE WORK PRODUCT?

A collective work product for a top leadership group is more difficult to identify than it is to define: *the tangible result of several members of a group applying different skills to produce a performance improvement not achievable by any one member alone.* It is important to reiterate that some kinds of valuable teaming efforts (as defined in the Glossary of Team Terms, Appendix A) do not require a set of collective work products. The "Magnificent Seven" women's gymnastics team that won the gold medal at the 100th Olympiad in Atlanta is a good example of an enabling team. Its sole challenge as a group was to obtain the best possible gymnastic performance from each individual team member. There was no collective work product beyond the individual scores achieved on individual events. A purist might call this a nonteam or a working group, reminding us that gymnastics is not a team sport, but that would fly in the face of how the term *team* is commonly used. Moreover, it would be naive to deny the value of the group's collective commitment not to let their teammates down, which constitutes a powerful source of motivation and support, and clearly warrants some kind of team label. It does not, however, constitute the kind of collective performance result that real teams obtain.

Real teams have the capacity for additional levels of performance above and beyond the personal best results achieved by each individual member. They apply their joint, complementary skills to work products that cannot be crafted by any one member of the group—and thereby add the value of those products to the results produced by members acting on their own. This combination of individual and collective work is what enables the real team to outperform its counterparts that focus only on individual results.

As we saw in Chapter 2, collective work products at the top are not as easy to come by as they are for teams down the line. The obvious focus of the top group on matters of vision, values, mission, strategy, and policy doesn't always lend itself to real work products for the members, as it did in the SmithKline Beecham situation. And, as indicated, the shaping of these important directional imperatives can be done within the normal organizational unit team. In fact, the best illustrations of real team performance tasks at the top center around the unpredictable. In 1993 Citicorp top executives formed a subteam effort around the redesign of their credit management process—after a major, unforeseen real estate collapse had created a financial crisis of major proportions across the industry. Four top executives functioned as a real team at Browning-Ferris, when raising several hundred million dollars in new financing became critical to their future growth. Sometimes the simple problem-solving task of just identifying the most critical team opportunities elsewhere in the organization constitutes a valid collective work product for the top organizational unit. But the fact remains that it is seldom easy for any top leadership group to carve out collective work products that match their skill mix and that also warrant the diversion of important increments of their time.

Figure 5.1 illustrates how collective work products explain the higher expected results of a real team versus a single-leader working group. The performance result of the single-leader working group is a simple combination of the individual results of each member. For example, the total of the individual scores of the "Magnificent Seven" won them the gold medal. Obviously, in gymnastics, there is no opportunity for collective work; hence, the group cannot achieve real team levels of performance.

The same can be said of the creatures in *The Spirit of Haida Gwaii* sculpture described in the Introduction—and in most forced team configurations at the top. Unless the group is chosen because of its joint work skills for a particular set of collective work products, it can achieve only the value of collective encouragement or apply what skills it does possess to whatever tasks it encounters that happen to fit those skills. Its team performance potential, therefore, remains limited by its predetermined membership configuration and fixed skill mix.

This description of collective work products can fit a wide variety of different work products that fall within the activity scope of would-be teams at the top. For example, many potential group activities at the top can be construed to fit the definition or not, depending on the

Figure 5.1
PERFORMANCE POTENTIAL

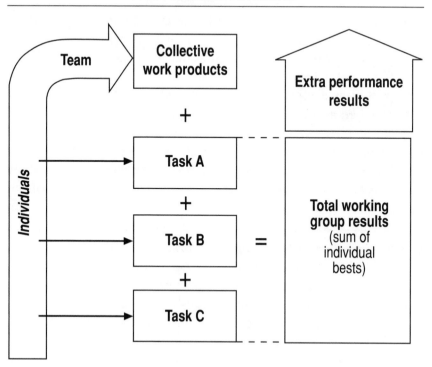

conditions under which they are pursued. The following illustrations describe sets of conditions that would qualify as a collective work product, along with examples of where the conditions were met and where they were not:

1. **Resolution of a key strategic issue.** Shaping overall strategy is normally a primary responsibility of the top leadership group of any business enterprise. Thus the specific resolution of a critical strategic issue is a natural collective work product for the group. It must, however, be an issue that requires problem solving through a collaborative group effort, and the group members must hold themselves accountable for the results, as was the case at Smith-Kline Beecham.

   Enron's decision to become a major player in the financing of natural gas facilities worldwide was such an issue. Ron Burns recalls the months of study, discussion, and debate among the top executives of the company before the resources were committed and a plan of attack established. Despite the company's strong culture of individual accountability, this issue was appropriately shared by the top leadership group. And its subsequent implementation was appropriately directed by single-leader working groups.

   Conversely, Prudential's well-publicized, but unsuccessful strategy to become a top-tier investment bank in the late 1980s was not formulated as a collective work product by the executive office of that company, although they reviewed and approved it on more than one occasion. George Ball, then CEO of Prudential-Bache, assumed individual responsibility for both shaping the strategy and directing its implementation. Although he received advice and counsel from the executive office of Prudential, he led the group to the decision. There was little collective work by the group.

2. **Redesign of a faulty management process.** Core process redesign (often called "reengineering") has become an invaluable way to achieve alignment and performance improvement throughout large corporations. Top leadership groups can bring about these important redesigns by assigning the task to internal task forces or staff specialists, by hiring external consultants, or by tackling the job themselves. Only in the latter case does it constitute a collective work product.

When the real estate lending crisis of the early 1990s hit Citicorp, it became apparent both internally and externally that the corporate credit management process with respect to real estate lending had been faulty. John Reed brought three forces to bear simultaneously on this issue: (1) he commissioned an internal task force to redesign the entire process; (2) he retained outside consultants to evaluate critical parts of the process; and (3) he convened his top seven executives to determine the key elements of a new process. Only the latter aspect of this three-pronged attack constituted a collective work product for the top leadership group.

When Mobil became concerned with its corporate overhead costs and staff service effectiveness, it commissioned a joint task-force/consultant effort called the Staff Redesign Project. It involved dozens of people full time for several months, resulted in recommendations that saved millions of dollars, and laid the groundwork for a new top leadership and organization approach. It did not, however, constitute a collective work product for the top leadership group, because very little of the real work was done by that group.

3. *Changing the organization structure.* Organization structure design is an important province of top leadership. Designs can be developed by staff advisors for senior executive group approval, they can be entirely the CEO's decision, or they can be the subject of intensive group problem-solving work. In the latter case, they can constitute valuable collective work products.

The earlier description of Gene Renna leading the Executive Office of Mobil in the redesign of the top organization structure is a good example of how structural designs can represent valuable collective work products. Even though Renna was given the assignment as an individual, he elected to pursue it by working in a real team mode with other members of Mobil's senior executive group. The new organization structure led to significant and important new assignments for over a dozen talented executives and significant improvements in the company's business performance. It was clearly a valuable collective work product.

Conversely, James Robinson, a former CEO of American Express, preferred to use organization structure as his individual means of aligning behaviors. For example, when he took over the leadership of the New York City Partnership from David Rockefeller, he spent several days working primarily with top staff advisors and consultants to redesign the top structure of the NYCP organization. It was a very well conceived new organization structure for the NYCP; however, it was not a collective work product of a senior leadership group.

4. ***Entry into a new market.*** New market entry is often very high on the risk/reward scale for top executive decisions; thus it can require the best collective judgment of top management. Since the market, by definition, is completely new to the enterprise, it is difficult to predict what will happen, and new market entry usually requires significant speculative investments. These decisions are often left to the CEO or delegated to staff analysts and a top marketing executive. Sometimes, however, they are shared among a small group of executives who bring their multiple skills and experience to bear in a joint decision for which they feel mutual accountability. Only in the latter case does the market entry constitute a collective work product for the top leadership group.

When Jim Rogers of GE's electrical motors business was considering entry into India, he set up a small team of top line and staff executives to evaluate the market, determine the alternative strategies, and design a plan that would accelerate the market entry. This plan did not constitute a collective work product for his 14-person top leadership group, even though they were part of the initial discussions and the final plan approval. It did, however, constitute a collective work product for the subteam that did the work.

5. ***Establishment of higher standards of performance.*** Performance aspirations and standards are clearly a primary responsibility of the CEO and his or her direct reports. CEOs often set these aspirations and standards themselves, usually in consultation with staff and outside advisors. Sometimes the corporate standards of performance are set by simply accumulating the standards set by the several different executives in charge of particular lines of business or subbusiness units. Occasionally, the CEO will convene a group of top-line executives to work together in shaping performance aspirations and establishing consistent standards across the organi-

zation. Only in the latter case (as we saw at SmithKline Beecham) does the effort constitute a collective work product for the leadership group—and then only for those executives who participated in the actual aspiration and standard-setting effort.

Lew Platt establishes Hewlett-Packard's aspirations and performance standards by working the territory with his top line of business leaders. It is a collective target which evolves as a combination of line-of-business aspirations with collective discussion and comparison across the businesses. Before the final numbers have been set, several top executives have worked with Platt to develop a common point of view. It is a collective work product of the top leadership group.

Shortly after Lou Noto was designated CEO of Mobil, he established a demanding performance aspiration and standard for the company: to achieve $3 billion in profit within four years. This had a dramatic impact on both the external market and the internal organization. Noto claims to have derived the magic number "on the back of an envelope" during one of his many global airplane trips, although it is well to observe that he is a very astute financial executive. Thus what might be a back-of-the-envelope calculation for Noto would be a pretty sophisticated analysis for the rest of us. However he came up with the $3 billion aspiration and performance standard, one thing is certain—it was not yet a collective work product for Mobil's top leadership group.

6. *Formulation of a communication strategy for major change.* Communication programs are often developed by staff and outside experts for major corporate organization and change efforts. While these efforts are always based on the inputs and thinking of the top executives, they may or may not require substantive work from them. If the key messages, audiences, and media are really developed by the staff—with or without the advice of the senior leadership group—they do not constitute a collective work product. The communication strategy for Mobil's 1996 corporate reorganization is an example of how such an effort can constitute substantive collective work by senior executives.

The Mobil reorganization involved a new line operating structure, a different corporate center philosophy, and a series of new leadership forums. The changes were extensive, and the implementation required a broad communication strategy based on a set of specific messages that were crafted by the Executive Office working together. For example, within their overall corporate theme of people, performance, and growth, they crafted the following (paraphrased) specifics:

- The new structure will create new performance opportunities and expectations for our highest-potential future leaders.
- The Executive and Opportunity Development Councils will accelerate the development and enhancement of our pool of future top leaders; similar efforts will focus on leaders at all levels.
- These changes will enhance the leadership focus on both growth and performance opportunities.
- We expect this organization to change as we learn more about how well it responds to our increasingly competitive situation.

These messages were not developed by either internal communication staff or external advisors. Each member of the Executive Office contributed to the ideas as well as the wording and worked together in thinking through how these key messages would serve as the basis for a broad-scale communication strategy to reach into all areas of the global enterprise. They also considered different ways to launch and reinforce these messages before involving others. A number of alternative messages were considered before the group settled on the final set. Subsequently, of course, a number of people were involved in converting the EO messages into a comprehensive communication program. The initial messages, however, were the core element of the program and as such clearly constituted an important collective work effort of the Executive Office.

The point of the preceding illustrations is not to suggest that collective work products are good or bad; rather, that they represent an option for real team behavior that deserves to be explicitly considered. The advantage of a collective work product is that it offers the opportunity for higher-performance results than would be obtained through the combination of individual work products. The disadvantage is that it requires more time, additional risks, and a different combination of leadership skills. Thus it represents an important tradeoff for top leadership groups to be able to make. It also represents the most tangible condition for determining if real team levels of performance are possible and relevant. Like mutual accountability and shifting leadership roles, the identification of collective work products becomes a good litmus test for identifying a potential real team opportunity.

UNIFYING THEMES AND INITIATIVES

Many top leadership groups stumble onto obvious collective work products that can enable some combination of their members to function in a team mode. When this happens infrequently and opportunistically, however, many similar opportunities are overlooked or simply pursued within the construct of a single-leader working group. As a result, the performance potential of the group is underrealized.

While there is no magic answer for correcting this shortfall, it helps if the group coalesces around a simple theme or integrating initiative. Such a theme can provide a focal point for the integration of what would otherwise be randomly picked collective work products; and the theme can and should change every so often. This is not the same thing as a corporate vision, mission, or strategy, although the short-term integrating theme should grow out of such overall directional imperatives for the enterprise.

In some respects, it is very similar to the "working vision" that we discovered to be guiding the efforts of real change leaders at middle and front-line levels. The change leaders' working vision is a very pragmatically determined phrase or message that grows out of their efforts to mobilize the resourcefulness of people around them. *Real Change Leaders* tells us that "a working vision consists of those few words—closer to five than fifty—that enable people to see clearly in their mind's eye where the change will take them, and why it matters."[8] The vision seldom is as meaningful to those outside the immediate working group, but those within that group find it to be memorable, motivating, and relevant to their change challenge. The following are three examples of working visions from *Real Change Leaders*, to clarify the notion:

- *"Eliminate what annoys our bankers and our customers"* was the theme that integrated the efforts of literally thousands of people at the Texas Commerce Bank in a year-long effort to streamline their organization and improve their performance by over $50 million.
- *"The one others copy"* energized dozens of asset management teams within Mobil's U.S. Exploration and Production (MEPUS) operation to achieve $300 million in profit improvements and move MEPUS from last to first among its benchmarked peer group of competitors.
- *"No graffiti"* evoked a clear, desirable image that enabled customers, employees, and politicians alike to track and motivate progress in the New York City Transit Authority's surprisingly successful effort to revitalize the city's subway system in the late 1980s and early 1990s.[9]

These are clear, concise messages that help real change leaders at middle-management levels to integrate the efforts of hundreds of people in a major change situation. This same kind of integrating theme has value in leadership groups at the top of large organizations—particularly with respect to optimizing the selection and pursuit of collective work products. We have already seen how the simple themes "Simply Better" and "Now We Are One" were used at Smith-Kline to integrate collective work products and teams. The following case examples illustrate how this worked with two different top leadership groups: the Executive Development Council at Mobil, and the top leadership group at Pall Corporation.

Mobil's Executive Development Council

Mobil's Executive Development Council (EDC) was an outgrowth of a natural team effort that was part of the extensive Staff Redesign Project (SRP) commissioned by Lou Noto shortly after he became CEO in 1994. The origin of the council, as described in Chapter 3, played a big part in its team performance over time. Because of the urgency associated with staffing the SRP's redesigned corporate center, several of the company's very best future executives were assigned to develop a more rigorous, fact-based, and balanced process of evaluating both the performance and the development needs of middle to upper managers. This one-time special evaluation project established the credibility of this kind of new process as the primary element of the company's high-priority efforts to accelerate the development of its overall leadership capacity.

Hence, when the Executive Development Council (EDC) became an ongoing part of Mobil's top leadership approach, it was natural that the group function in the same team mode as its predecessor group. As such, the Council developed and applied a number of high-impact, collective work products. For example,

- *A new leadership development profile.* They completely redesigned the criteria and evidence required for determining the leadership accomplishments of middle and upper managers. A number of similar descriptors and criteria had been developed throughout the company, but no one had yet integrated the best of them into a comprehensive, prioritized template. Moreover, the profiles used in the past had placed primary emphasis on evaluations, whereas this one placed the emphasis on development as well.

- *A more rigorous evaluation process.* They developed a new process for the senior leadership group to use in evaluating candidates for top positions (the top 100). This process not only included 360-degree evaluation information, it also required intensive interviews by senior executives plus fact-based information on candidates that went well beyond normal human resource process evaluations. Although this was initially applied only to the upper levels of management, it established the pattern and model for similar process changes throughout the organization.

- *A new opportunity development and assignment matching process.* They worked out a completely different pattern for the Executive Office and the EDC to follow in expanding the leadership capacity of the company. A parallel group called the Opportunity Development Council was established. Its task was to surface development opportunities within both the formal and the informal structure of the company. These were then compared to the EDC's leadership profile work, and people were matched with development situations on a much more consistent and thorough basis.

At first, the collective work opportunities were obvious, and both of these councils did a good job of deciding whether to pursue them in a team mode or not. As their efforts evolved, however, they coalesced around a few simple messages and integrating initiatives that enabled them to better optimize the balance between collective work and individual tasks.

The first of these, and perhaps the most powerful, can be described as *"Our primary focus is development, not evaluation."* Although the group did not consciously shape this as their theme, that is what it became. Like working visions for change leaders, it evolved out of the work. Paying more attention to development may appear to be a simple shift in emphasis, but it provided much more meaning for members of the EDC. It meant they were really trying to help their colleagues achieve higher levels of personal performance, rather than simply evaluating their relative success or failure. It also shifted the balance of the collective work into the development side of the equation. Finally, it enabled them to actually identify collective work products that they might otherwise have overlooked, such as the new leadership development template and the specific pursuit of diverse development opportunities. Much of the straight evaluation work could now be delegated to organization unit leaders and teams in the formal structure, whereas the council's work and discussions could concentrate on problem solving for high-potential development needs.

Thus the focus provided by this theme had two benefits for members of the EDC: (1) it helped them to integrate and optimize the value of their collective work products, and (2) it energized them as a group, providing more natural opportunities for them to function in a real team mode.

Pall Corporation's European Foothold Theme

The interjection of the right theme or initiative at the right time can do a lot for energizing a leadership group, as well as for its team performance. This synopsis of Pall Corporation's dramatic development from an idea in Dr. David Pall's chemical lab work to a global enterprise serves to illustrate that point. Pall is now the world's leading supplier of filtration and separation products, with annual sales of around $1 billion and a pretax profit margin of over 20 percent. From

1970 to 1980, Pall showed the highest total return to shareholders of any Fortune 1000 industrial company. Its growth slowed in the 1980s due to cuts in the defense industry (a major customer group). Still, Pall's leading-edge technology coupled with its expansion into international markets has kept the company well ahead of the competition.

It starts as a venture story and, like most venture stories, represents a special situation with regard to teams at the top. Almost by definition, a new venture is blessed with the two most important ingredients for team performance: a clear, compelling sense of purpose (namely, survival!) and an incredible level of personal commitment by the founding partners (individual net worths and pride are at stake). New ventures are often led by real teams at the top—at least for a while.

The Pall story, however, is much more than that of a new business venture. In particular, it illustrates real team efforts at the top within the context of a broader set of top leadership challenges. Its founders functioned as a real team at several critical junctures over more than four decades of growth, performance, and change. In the 1950s, when David Pall and Abraham Krasnoff realized the uniqueness of their product offerings (basically, technologically superior filters and filtering systems), they became firmly committed to making Pall Corporation a global leader, because, as Krasnoff described the rationale to us, "no successful enterprise can sustain itself long unless it pursues a niche philosophy—and that philosophy will inevitably demand global capabilities if the business is to achieve its potential."

This "global leader" vision for the company, however, did not take on the power of a simple integrating theme for the top leadership group until Maurice Hardy joined the party some ten years down the road. In the interim, of course, there were many randomly pursued collective work efforts, some of which produced team performance in short bursts. For example, Krasnoff and Pall were joined by Sidney Krakauer, a chemist whom Pall knew in his earlier life on the infamous atomic bomb Manhattan Project, and Chesterfield Seibert, an engineer who sat on the Pall Board well after his active work at the company. This leadership group did not always get along well, and its most significant collective work products were in subteam efforts. Krakauer and Pall were experts in the same field whose strongly held views often differed. Krasnoff's efforts at amelioration between the two, however, plus the life-or-death nature of the venture, sustained the commitment necessary to keep the group functioning as an effective working group, though seldom as a real team. One of the early life-or-death issues was the absence of critical manufacturing capability—no one in the leadership group had that kind of competence until Henry Petronis, from one of Pall's subcontractors, signed on. Now they were a reasonably balanced working group of five: Pall, Krasnoff, Seibert, Krakauer, and Petronis. On big problems of companywide significance they grudgingly came together because they knew they had to; functional issues or issues restricted in scope, however, were resolved by subgroups.

It wasn't until Maurice Hardy joined the group in 1962 that real team performance began to forge a new leadership group. Hardy, who came to the group through an acquisition, had the critical international know-how that could bring the vision to fruition. In fact, Krasnoff claims that he and Pall really saw Hardy's European capability as the primary benefit of the acquisition. Successful European entry became the watchword and theme that continually focused their team efforts. As Krasnoff later recalled, "I went over and met this guy (recommended by a customer), and we hit it off . . . we acquired his little company to become our link to Europe. The critical issue was . . . his knowledge as a businessman in Europe." And it was at that point that the global vision became a practical, integrative theme for the top leadership group: *"establish a foothold in Europe by the end of the decade."* This sharply focused theme not only surfaced collective work products, but also gave more shape to the working approach within the leadership team, which soon narrowed to a group of three.

Fortunately, they represented the essential competencies required, because the obstacle of distance kept collective working time to a minimum. They were forced to meet quarterly, in intensive two-day working and problem-solving sessions, and to find all kinds of ways to communicate across the water. Krasnoff recalls countless trips abroad, and Hardy remembers the somewhat animated quarterly meetings and the hundreds of handwritten notes. Obviously, they lacked the advantages of today's low-cost fax and electronic mail. Nonetheless, Hardy, whose colleagues to this day laud his communication skills, established an early pattern of extensive communication which continually reinforced the theme of establishing a European foothold and thereby enabled the group to do real work together across great geographic distances. As captured in *The Winning Performance,* Krasnoff's relentless communication efforts were also critical in keeping the theme alive and well.

> Krasnoff kept in constant contact with his team through very frequent personal meetings, phone calls and group interactions. He broke through barriers by dropping in unannounced to meetings. His manner was very upbeat and unthreatening, which also helped promote constructive conflict.[10]

By 1990 the company had become the leading fine filter provider in Europe and Japan as well as the United States.[11] In 1996, 60 percent of Pall's sales were derived outside of the Western Hemisphere, with about 40 percent from Europe and 20 percent from Asia. It now has 17 international offices and plants worldwide. In 1989 Queen Elizabeth II made Maurice Hardy a Commander of the Order of the British Empire, and in 1990, President George Bush awarded Dr. David Pall the National Medal of Technology.

Many things stand out from this synopsis of Pall Corporation's global success. The most important, however, is how powerful their simple theme was in surfacing team opportunity at the top. When the missing ingredient of European know-how arrived in the form of Maurice Hardy, the broad global vision became tightly focused around the simple, pragmatic theme of European market entry. That theme served as a powerful motivating and coalescing beacon for both shaping the top leadership team's working approach and integrating a number of collective work products.

As this story illustrates, a simple theme can be much more effective in coalescing real team efforts than a broad, all-encompassing vision for three fundamental reasons:

1. It constitutes something that the senior executives—as a group—can focus their combined attention and work on together.

2. It surfaces more definitive collective work products and helps to tie such products together into a more cohesive effort within the senior group.

3. It does not require a great deal of shaping or "wordsmithing," because it emerges out of the real issues and is framed in simple language.

Obviously, a simple theme is not necessarily the only answer to enabling collective work products or to achieving a balanced senior leadership approach that integrates both team and nonteam efforts. It is, however, much more than just a useful notion, particularly when it comes about from working the key issues. It provides an essential focal point for the collective work of senior leadership groups.

MAINTAINING COLLECTIVE MOMENTUM

But how do you keep the momentum going? For a leadership group that derives its team performance only from major, unpredictable events and randomly pursued collective work products, that is a good question. Of course, the leadership groups of most high-performing companies spend little of their time worrying about a shortage of unpredictable major events; quite the opposite, in fact. And there are plenty of possible collective work products lying around to tantalize those with unfulfilled team instincts and desires. So maybe this is only a problem for the leaders of mediocre-performing enterprises.

If so, why do the leadership groups at the top of some of our better-performing companies lose their momentum after a few short years? Harvey Golub, CEO of American Express, once wrote me a provocative memo entitled "Why Leaders Lose," which dealt with that topic at length. Golub's view at the time—and I suspect he still holds it—was that leaders lose because they fail to stay out in front of their marketplace and become complacent or comfortable with leadership and organization approaches that worked well for them in the past. Put another way, they become wedded to their personal favorite formulas for winning a game that has changed on them.

The best CEOs are not wedded to one formula, no matter how well it might have worked for them. They do not believe that the dynamics of the marketplace alone will be enough to keep their executives sharp. Nor do they believe that executives' natural leadership instincts will ensure the actions necessary to keep the company in front of its competition. They know that staying ahead of the competition demands consistent attention to redesigning both strategies and leadership approaches. They also know it is essential to expand leadership capacity ahead of the need across the enterprise.

Some might question whether or not there is a risk of creating a "flavor of the month" perception through excessive refocusing and shifting of the senior leadership group's purpose and approach to better address different performance issues. The question has relevance only when such shifts are not directly related to real business issues and key opportunities. Moreover, it is important that the overall "leadership approach" be perceived as flexible and adaptive to both marketplace and workplace changes. In this context, a responsive leadership group could hardly be accused of "flavor of the month" behavior.

The secret to momentum and performance within the team at the top of any enterprise is to keep refocusing the group's performance purpose and identifying the specific issues and work products that purpose suggests. This means launching new initiatives, shaping new working themes, and rebalancing the team, working group, and individual elements of the approach. If you start to feel comfortable with the way your leadership group at the top is functioning, it's probably time to change it.

Sometimes this discussion prompts the question of when to disband the team at the top. This question derives from the either/or mindset addressed earlier. The entire premise of this book is based on the importance of integrating team and nonteam modes of behavior within an ongoing senior leadership group. *Senior leadership groups (so-called teams at the top) do not disband—they shift into and out of team modes of behavior to fit the performance tasks at hand.*

CONCLUSION: DON'T LEAVE IT TO CHANCE

Meredith Willson's award-winning Broadway musical, *The Music Man*, contains a scene in which the male lead, Professor Harold Hill (originally and memorably played by Robert Preston), puts together a barbershop quartet of local talent. As the group gains enthusiasm and confidence from its early efforts singing together, Professor Hill slyly observes, "they will never be out of each other's sight again."

A more recent illustration of this same cohesion occurred with the filming of "The Three Tenors," a TV special in which three world-famous tenors, José Carreras, Placido Domingo, and Luciano Pavarotti, present a brilliant program of operatic arias as a trio. Operatic tenors, of course, are noteworthy in their strong preference for solo work. Yet afterwards, each goes out of his way to comment on how personally rewarding he found singing in the trio to be. Not surprisingly, their collective efforts produced a program (comprised of "collective work products") that received the highest acclaim from audience and critics alike.

Top leadership groups that do real work together are much like musical groups that sing or play together. As they gain a firsthand appreciation for the talent each possesses, they develop mutual respect for one another, along with a strong conviction about the value of what they can accomplish together. Unless the group continues to do substantive work together, however, it will lose the tangible value from the collective work products.

The collective work of teams can be particularly powerful in situations where the marketplace situation is difficult to predict, where no single member of the leadership group has the answer, and where the performance upside of responding differently is very high. Leaving the identification of such situations to chance means that many potential team opportunities will go unrecognized—and that executive leadership disciplines and instincts will prevail over team instincts and disciplines. In other words, you will not be making the best use of all the performance tools at your disposal.

Some leadership groups, of course, err in the opposite way, by attempting to forge a team around performance opportunities that do not call for a team approach. In fact, the increasing emphasis that team proponents place on "team-based organizations" creates real frustrations as top leadership groups try to rationalize good executive leadership instincts into time-consuming team building that has no performance purpose. Catalyzing real team performance at the top does not mean replacing executive leadership with executive teams; it means being rigorous about the distinction between opportunities that require single-leader efforts and those that require team efforts—and applying the discipline that fits.

Leaving collective performance issues at the top to chance will result in suboptimal performance contributions by any leadership group—as well as important missed opportunities for higher performance by the company. *Every top leadership group should, at a minimum, be able to identify and prioritize the handful of team opportunities (six to eight) that offer the most performance potential in the company—even* if they don't involve top executives. It is increasingly unlikely, however, that one or more of those opportunities will not benefit from some kind of top executive leadership, sponsorship, or membership. Paradoxically, when leadership groups make a serious effort as a group to identify the company's highest-potential team opportunities, it invariably constitutes a collective work product, and in the process, the group functions as a real team.

Making Key Tradeoffs Consciously

IN THE WORLD OF POLITICS, any group qualifies as a "team." Neither size, nor purpose, nor configuration matters; any collective gathering of more than two people with anything in common is likely to be labeled a "team." Moreover, the label can be applied by the press, the opposition, or the group itself. Togetherness of any dimension seems to constitute a valid political team.

The presidential race of 1996, like those before it, provided ample evidence of the carefree use of the term. Both tickets were frequently referred to as "teams," just as new CEO corporate leadership groups are. Jack Kemp's football background led to a multitude of clever and not-so-clever jibes about who was the quarterback of the "team." In every presidential election, the press invariably expresses a great deal of concern about whether or not members of the so-called team can have opposite views, opinions, and philosophies on key issues. The question itself illustrates the carefree use of the term. Although it may be valid with respect to a presidential ticket, it is hardly relevant with respect to a performance team, where conflicting points of view provide the essential "spice in the chili."

Presidential campaigns, however, are one of the more conspicuous examples of the misuse of the term. As a campaign gathers momentum, we hear much about each party's core team, although the precise membership of these teams isn't always clear. Then there are the potential "subteams" for each ticket: press, speech writing, and cabinet screening teams. Frequently, one or more members of these so-called teams are replaced as a result of shifting poll results or a member's missteps. As the actual elections draw near, journalists begin to probe a bit into each candidate's likely cabinet choices. Who would the president-elect choose for his team at the top? Of course, it's always a little murky as to whether these references to a prospective "team at the top" include only the vice president–elect, the rest of the cabinet, or maybe some special subset. And, naturally, after the election there is always plenty of speculation about the "kitchen cabinet" possibilities, because that will probably turn out to be the actual team at the top.

Politics may be a world of murky and imprecise language, but when it comes to team terminology, the business world is equally murky. Consequently, the carefree use of the term *team* is neither surprising nor disturbing to most people—it's simply standard practice for politicians, businessmen and journalists. We have become as unconcerned about the careless use of team descriptors as we are with many other aspects of political or business legerdemain.

For those of us who care about team performance, however, it strikes at the heart of the problem for would-be teams at the top. As emphasized in the Introduction, those who are careless in their language about teams invariably reflect the same lack of rigor in how they think about team performance opportunity—and how they apply the basic elements of team discipline. A great many top leadership challenges are simply not team opportunities. Referring to them as such is not only misleading to observers of the so-called team, but it can lead those so labeled to worry about and waste time trying to become more teamlike. In addition, many top leadership challenges that constitute real team opportunities simply do not require or warrant active participation by all who have been designated as "on the team." Only infrequently does a formal "team at the top" function in a single-team mode that includes all the formal members.

Whatever leads a potential team to be careless about its mode of behavior (not making a clear distinction as to the leader's role) and membership (assuming that a member's skill set is defined by her job title) doesn't matter. The net result is still suboptimal levels of performance for the group. This is particularly true for teams at the top because of the special constraints and conditions that surround a senior leadership group. This chapter is devoted to describing how teams at the top can make more effective use of the modes and membership configurations available to them. It addresses the three basic tradeoffs that come into play with any would-be team at the top as it considers its various small group options:

1. *The time tradeoff.* Performance versus speed (value of collective results versus the time required to pursue those results)

2. *The capability tradeoff.* Complementary skill mix versus formal "position influence" (specific task capability versus official job responsibility)

3. *The capacity tradeoff.* Leadership capacity versus leadership clarity (shifting the leader role among the members versus maintaining a single leader)

THE TIME TRADEOFF: PERFORMANCE VERSUS SPEED

There is little question that time has a disproportionate influence on team performance at the top. On the one hand, it takes time for executives to learn when and how to apply the discipline of teams. Consequently, many senior leadership groups avoid the issue altogether by maintaining they cannot afford the time. On the other hand, those who believe that team performance is worth the extra time can easily spend too much time working with a "good plow [in the] wrong field,"[1] pursuing a team when the speed and efficiency of a nonteam makes better sense.

Donald Hambrick's work cited earlier suggests that it can take two years or more for such issues to moderate. To illustrate how difficult these tradeoffs can be, this section draws on one of the more remarkable entrepreneurial success stories of the 1980s—Ben & Jerry's Homemade, Inc.—arguably the creator of the super-premium ice cream market. The company was conceived and built by two close friends, who have always aspired to what others might consider impossible, if not naive: a company whose performance would be determined as much by its social and community contributions as by its market and shareholder gains. This has not been an easy aspiration to pursue, much less achieve.

The Early Years at Ben & Jerry's

In the beginning, this was a story of venture survival—when team efforts by the founders were virtually a given. Ever since Ben Cohen and Jerry Greenfield decided to turn the active leadership of the company over to others, however, real team efforts at the top have become increasingly difficult. In fact, since Cohen formally retired as CEO in 1989, the company has had four different CEOs, only one of whom was in serious pursuit of team performance at the top (and he left within two years). The Ben & Jerry's episode that follows is particularly instructive because it illustrates how critical time tradeoffs can be in determining team performance at the top. It also captures the difficulty of trying to obtain team performance in the face of an unyielding individual executive leadership mindset—particularly during the early stages of a new leadership group that lacks real team experience.

As this unusual company entered the 1990s, the storm clouds of competitive intensity and leadership transitions began to threaten its past performance record. The early years of struggle, growth, and achievement are entertainingly chronicled in the book *Ben & Jerry's: The Inside Scoop* by Fred "Chico" Lager,[2] who served as president and CEO through some of Ben & Jerry's more exciting growth years.

Like most successful new ventures, it was a remarkable journey, which created a powerful bond between the founders, Ben Cohen and Jerry Greenfield, and some of their board members. However, there is little doubt that Ben Cohen emerged during that journey as the natural marketing leader (some say genius) of the enterprise, and continued in that mode throughout a CEO parade of four successors. The first was Chico Lager, who points out in his book:

> The prospect of Ben taking a less active role in the business was both encouraging and disconcerting. There was no doubt that Ben had been the driving force who was most responsible for the company's success. . . . We were daunted by the prospect of turning our marketing and image over to a total stranger in the hopes that he or she could duplicate Ben's success.[3]

Ben's and Jerry's personal roles cannot be separated from the unique set of values that distinguishes the company not only from its competitors, but probably from most other corporations. The seriousness of their social service intent makes their three-part mission truly unique: to make the highest-quality products; to create economic value for their shareholders and employees; *and to improve quality of life in their local, national, and international communities.* Ben, Jerry, and their colleagues on the board, as well as most members of the top management team, believe strongly that the company's business performance (market and financial) is positively and integrally linked to the company's social and community performance. As Ben and Jerry are fond of saying, "You can do good by doing good." They staunchly maintain that a good part of the company's competitive advantage stems from its social values.

A Time-Urgent Environment

The founders continue to occupy a special place in the informal leadership construct of the company, regardless of how the formal organization structure and job responsibilities are defined. Lager's book makes clear the many positive and negative aspects of those special roles. One of the most notable is the sense of urgency they engender with respect to the company's business and social performance. Having created a unique enterprise, they are determined to see it flourish. Ben in particular has no patience for shortfalls on either the business or social dimension, whatever the cause. Thus speed is of disproportionate importance in any improvement program. And, because the company competes in a market that places the highest premium on speed and frequency of new product introductions, time urgency becomes doubly pressing. For these reasons, the tradeoff between time and performance at Ben & Jerry's is a critical one, and its impact on team efforts at the top has been significant.

Figure 6.1 is a simple illustration of the time and performance tradeoffs between single-leader working group and real team configurations. It is a company-specific application of the conceptual chart in Chapter 2 (Figure 2.1). This tradeoff is difficult at the top of most large organizations, because of both the premium on executive time and the upside potential of real team performance. As a result, leadership groups that can shift easily from a working group mode to a team mode (and back again) are likely to avail themselves of higher-performance results and more leadership capacity over time. It is, however, a difficult mindset to acquire, as top executives are much more comfortable with the orderliness of the single-leader working group.

This was particularly true at Ben & Jerry's, because: (1) the company's earlier experience with empowerment teams at lower levels was not a positive one; and (2) Ben's own experience in running the company reinforced his belief in the value of a strong, decisive leader at the top. The environment could hardly be described as "team-friendly" at the top to begin with—and the time urgency of the competitive performance situation further complicated any and all team efforts at the top.

In fact, between 1994 and 1996, the senior leadership group moved through three different positions with regard to time and performance

Figure 6.1
THE SPEED TRADEOFF: *PERFORMANCE VERSUS TIME*

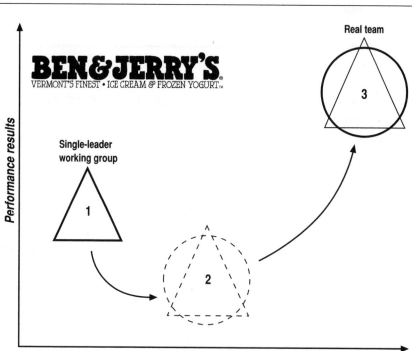

tradeoffs. Prior to 1994, the senior leaders functioned pretty much as a single-leader working group (symbol 1 in Figure 6.1). In the early months of CEO Robert Holland's efforts to shape a new team, they slipped into a less efficient learning mode while developing the skills and commitment to work more as a team (symbol 2). In the end, as they learned to differentiate better between team and nonteam tasks, they began to achieve real team levels of performance (symbol 3). This transition took months longer than expected, largely because most of the group was new to the company, as well as unaccustomed to working together, at least as a potential team.

Given their history and the competitive dynamics of their industry, it was not surprising that Cohen and most of his board found the senior group's delay in coming together to be frustrating, if not intolerable. They were expecting a "turnaround time frame."

Shaping a New Top Team

In 1994, following a nationwide search that drew national media attention, Robert Holland was retained as CEO. Both of his predecessors had functioned primarily in a single-leader working group mode. Holland had a diverse record of consulting and business recovery situations. And, although he recognized the unique and difficult founder constraints at Ben & Jerry's, he could not resist the challenge. Moreover, he truly shared the strong social values of the founders, which in retrospect he probably misread as being "team-friendly." In addition, his view of the business challenge was based on a thoughtful, fact-based, and strategic view of how the company needed to change to become a major global competitor. He believed that aspiration would require the pursuit of fundamental changes in the culture and capabilities of the organization over an extended period of time.

While Cohen was uncomfortable with the time frame, he agreed that the most important priority was putting together a new top leadership group (not necessarily a team, however). This became a major point of difference between the two leaders. Cohen favored the strong, decisive action that "executive leadership discipline" suggests. Holland favored an approach that would create more teamwork and real team capability among the senior group. His attitude was very similar to that of Richard Olson, the CEO of Champion described in

Chapter 1: "One of us is not as good as all of us." As a result, he envisioned that the critical work at the top of the organization would be pursued collectively by members of the Office of the CEO (OCEO), not just by the CEO. He strongly encouraged teamwork among this top management group by giving the OCEO members an equal voice in meetings, in communications, and in decisions. Although he realized this was time consuming, he believed it would pay off in more leadership capacity over time. Instead of the traditional CEO roles of chief figurehead, agenda controller, and solo decision maker, he took on the roles of team opportunity spotter, theme shaper, and skill mix manager while maintaining the authority to revert to the traditional CEO role when necessary.

Cohen found this approach to be increasingly troublesome. For several months the leadership group struggled to develop a working approach that fit both their skills and the performance challenges they faced. This would-be "team at the top" was not only missing key members for critical leadership roles, but many of the members were new to their jobs—and they had much to learn about the business, the culture, and one another. The "in your face" style of interaction throughout the company used up a great deal of their time and energy. They were a classic example of a new group groping for cohesion and alignment, which Hambrick highlights in his material on the fragmentation referred to earlier:

> A new CEO often injects enough new members or simply enough new tension and uncertainty into the team to essentially throw it into a social disequilibrium. Patterns of communication, exchange and influence are disrupted, often even among continuing members.[4]

In short, early in a CEO's tenure the top group tends not to form a coherent information-processing or decision making body. Symbol 2 in Figure 6.1 indicates their relative position in terms of the performance and time tradeoffs the new group was making.

By early 1996, this partially formed senior leadership group was facing "system overload." They had identified close to 40 different initiatives and issues for top-priority action. As a result, they were feeling more than a little discouraged with the team aspects and time tradeoffs of their group. Everyone knew that the business was challenged and that things were not moving fast enough or in fully consistent directions. Yet there was little agreement as to the causes of the problem or the best immediate strategy for moving forward. The list of urgent issues and actions was overwhelming.

Making Better Tradeoffs

In the midst of this, the OCEO met in an informal and open discussion of how to make better tradeoffs with respect to the time demands on members of the group. The meeting included Holland and most of his direct reports—namely, Bruce Bowman, Frances Rathke, Elizabeth Bankowski, and Jerry Welsh. Welsh had been retained to direct the marketing operations until a permanent top marketing executive could be recruited. Although the group was clear about the multitude of challenges it faced, it was unclear about the relative priorities. Thus virtually everything became high priority. Group agendas and individual activities of every executive were overloaded with high-priority tasks; time quickly became the overwhelmingly scarce resource for every member of the team. As Welsh said, "we have no time to do anything but get after these—I don't see how it helps to get everyone's opinions on things that only one of us knows."

Clearly (to borrow Mark Childers' phrase from Chapter 1), they were looking for someone to help "make a clearing in the forest." Richard Hackman, in his book on *Groups That Work (and Those That Don't)*, articulates an important cause of their frustration, which he has found in other top groups:

> . . . when there was chronic uncertainty about which issues were in the team's domain and which would remain the prerogative of the [individual] executive, difficulties emerged. Team members could accept whatever boundaries . . . [were] established as long as they were clear.[5]

In my view, the group members were caught between the two classic extreme assumptions—team versus hierarchy—about how they should work together. In fact, they could rarely find a time when more than two or three of them could be in the same room together. Some believed, as Welsh, that each executive must simply get on with his or her own priority tasks. To that end, they wanted the CEO to take a stronger leadership role in resolving many cross-functional issues or corporate-level decisions. Others believed they needed the extra time together clarifying priorities. Bowman likens it all to an old carnival game, where you're given a hammer and expected to bang down on the heads of wooden dummies that pop up randomly through a board full of holes. It's impossible to keep up with the bobbing heads. So it was with the "top-priority" action demands on each and every member of the OCEO—impossible to keep up with individual needs, much less devote time to collective work.

On the other hand, the group readily acknowledged that several of the issues warranted collective action and was committed to Holland's desire to shape real team capability at the top to address such issues. Compressed time frames, however, made this course seem impossible—particularly given the pressures and heightened sense of urgency all were feeling from the marketplace as well as the founders. It was a classic conundrum of not having enough time even to find ways of making better use of the time available.

Finding the Time "On the Fly"

Nonetheless, the group concluded it must somehow find the time for both individual and collective work. After much discussion, Holland got the members to commit to meeting together once a week. This implied a major departure from their normal frantic, individual telephone and one-on-one pattern. Schedule overloads, travel demands, and even personal lifestyles (three members did not even live in Vermont!) would not yield easily to the weekly meeting proposal.

In their next meeting, Holland helped the OCEO shift more into a potential team mode by building consensus and commitment around shared goals. He led them through a group process to prioritize the 40 different "top-priority" initiatives. The group debated each initiative's relative urgency and importance to Ben & Jerry's success. The group assigned its individual members responsibility for each of the new top priorities and, in some cases, formed subteams to tackle them.

The weekly sessions, however, often were not "real work" sessions. Instead, the time was devoted to venting pent-up feelings, creating trust, sharing information, and getting to know one another. As a result, the discussions were extremely open and animated. Rathke recalls that "in our meetings, you might feel terrified, but you're never bored!" Much like the early meetings of the senior leaders at Champion, the group had to spend time just developing a common language for discussing the issues. As Liz Bankowski points out in retrospect, "Initially, our group dialogues took valuable time from our individual responsibilities. Nonetheless, it was essential that we spend that time bringing one another to a common level of understanding of the business and the competitive situation that we faced." Most importantly, these meetings "teed-up" the real work that went on between meetings—sometimes by individuals in coordination with others, and sometimes in real subteams or working groups of two or three. In other words, the real work of the OCEO was being done mostly "on the fly" between meetings, telephonically, electronically, and in smaller groups. In fact, some of their most important accomplishments can be described as simply "double- or triple-teaming" another member to change an unconstructive bias or approach and thereby reach a more common understanding and level of commitment consistent with the others. For example, they "gang-tackled" Welsh in this way to convince him that sharing his issues with the group had value for him as well as the others—and it wasn't easy!

Within the OCEO, subteams began to make increasing sense, sometimes including people outside the OCEO. Unfortunately, all of the discussions and interactions were taking up time that Cohen thought could be better spent taking action of some kind. Although he recognized that a major cause of this frenetic, time-consuming work pattern was the urgency imposed by the many diverse activities and priorities, his patience was running out.

By the middle of 1996, both Cohen and Holland recognized that this had become a no-win situation for both of them. In September, they announced that Holland's major contributions in strategy, plant rationalization, and market positioning were producing an implementation challenge that would require different CEO skills and interests. Despite the fact that Holland had maintained from the start that he was in a transition role as CEO, his resignation was an unexpected blow to his team.

In retrospect, Bowman observes that "one way or another, Bob Holland had succeeded in shaping a very cohesive top leadership group that could function effectively without him," when that became necessary. Sooner than expected, it had become necessary. Rather than demoralize the OCEO team, however, it created the kind of unexpected event that sometimes enables a senior group to "rise to the occasion" and function as a real team. These were exactly the words that Liz Bankowski used in describing the situation to an anxious group of board members in mid-September.

OCEO Dynamics

The group functioned in a variety of different modes during the critical leadership transition. As Bowman observed, the team had already learned to function on its own. Instinctively, it worked mostly in small subgroups and informal interactions in ways that fit the tasks it faced— again, with much of the real work being done "on the fly." From the original list of nearly 40 key issues, only the top 10 ever got much attention.

The group's weekly time together had become a fairly unstructured event that all attended—even Jerry Welsh, the group's favorite maverick, reluctantly conceded that it was worth the time. Originally, the primary value was that of bringing everyone to a common level of understanding about the business and the issues. As this need became less critical, the meetings focused more on tasks and issues that the group needed to talk about together. Sometimes they would work a particular issue as a group. For example, they shaped a set of common "talking points" for all executives and board members to follow in answering press questions about the succession. More often, however, the discussions simply served to identify where individuals or subgroups needed to get together for real work between the scheduled OCEO meetings. A very critical pricing decision in the fall of 1996, for example, was initially worked through mostly by Bowman, Rathke, and Welsh. Bowman later worked it through with all members of the OCEO. "I didn't want anyone coming back to me if things went wrong to say 'I really didn't agree with that after all.'"

Perhaps the most interesting indication of the common level of commitment and respect among the OCEO came when the board unexpectedly asked Bowman to become COO and run the company until Holland's replacement could be identified. Bowman wasn't expecting that decision and asked the board to let his team—the OCEO—jointly decide how his new role should be positioned and announced. It was a clear recognition by Bowman of how strongly the group viewed its collective responsibility, and how he wanted to ensure they remained "all in the same boat" when it came to company performance. At long last—perhaps too long in light of the company's performance issues—the group was recognizing when and how to function as a real team (symbol 3 in Figure 6.1).

Comparing with Champion

Ben & Jerry's team efforts at the top provide an interesting contrast with Champion's recent effort, described in Chapter 1. Both groups faced similar hurdles: a change in CEO and other top executive positions, strong pressures to improve performance and build new capabilities for the future, as well as the need to strengthen some core capabilities, such as marketing. Yet the new leadership group at Champion had a much smoother and faster transition to actually functioning in a real team mode. Table 6.1 compares the two to identify the more important reasons why Champion's senior group was able to get a jump on team effectiveness much sooner than Ben & Jerry's.

The OCEO at Ben & Jerry's did what it had to do to fill in the gaps and make a leadership approach in transition work. In retrospect, it struggled hard to find common ground between functioning as a real team, a single-leader working group, and a coordinated collection of individuals. As Table 6.1 indicates, the OCEO struggled between the two extremes. Nonetheless, it got the job done under stringent time urgency and difficult external conditions—without the benefit of the team experience base and strong team support at Champion. There are some important lessons here for teams at all levels:

1. Time urgency and unclear priorities create difficult obstacles for real team efforts. A senior group can seldom work in a real team mode unless it agrees that certain team tasks and goals are more important to the organization's performance than the individual responsibilities and goals of its members.

Table 6.1

COMPARING TWO SENIOR LEADERSHIP TEAM EFFORTS

Factors that Differentiate	CHAMPION INTERNATIONAL CORPORATION	BEN & JERRY'S HOMEMADE, Inc.	COMMENTS
1. Overall company experience with teams	Several years of learning in both mill operations and staff support departments	Early efforts with involvement teams not positive; recent production teams working well	B&J had much less real team performance experience to draw or build on
2. Senior group's prior experience with teams	All 8 members had worked with real teams and SLWGs in several situations	Few had worked with real teams; SLWGs not differentiated	Champion leaders knew exactly what to expect and how to react
3. Continuing top support over time	Former CEO worked to build team capabilities among successor candidates; board was supportive	Former CEO support very tentative regarding team efforts; board unfamiliar, unsure, and impatient	Champion had a much stronger cadre of true believers at the top over a longer time frame
4. Skills of team members	Most had worked in other functions; each had a set of complementary, distinctive skills	Critical skills were missing, and few members had cross-function experience	B&J had critical skill gaps—both functional and team
5. Purpose and goals	Clear and consistent among all members	Priorities among team members varied a lot	Champion leaders knew each other and their business
6. Working style	Early focus on creating common language and understanding; strong fact base	"In your face" style; lots of debate on opinions with limited fact base	Champion had two years of "learning together" before attempting team performance

Table 6.1 (continued)
COMPARING TWO SENIOR LEADERSHIP TEAM EFFORTS

Factors that Differentiate	CHAMPION INTERNATIONAL CORPORATION	BEN & JERRY'S HOMEMADE, Inc.	COMMENTS
7. Early work products	Knew what to look for and readily identified collective work products	Did not differentiate between types of work products	B&J lacked a clear understanding of collective work products
8. Time spent working together	One to two days each week working as a group; had worked together for years prior	Difficult to find time for weekly work sessions; hadn't known each other long	Time pressures at B&J, as well as "system overload," virtually precluded working together
9. Apparent mutual accountability	Clear almost from the beginning—thanks to two-year transition process	Not clear until they confronted an unexpected crisis	The performance crisis at B&J forged the group together for the first time

2. Understanding the value of *both* real teams and single-leader working groups can increase the flexibility and options available to any leadership group. It is difficult to develop that understanding from scratch without a base of real team experience to draw on.

3. Doing real work together need not mean all together and in meetings. Working "on the fly" and through multiple interaction vehicles (such as phone, fax, and email) can create high-value collective work products. Nonetheless, finding the time to do real work together matters a great deal.

4. Team efforts at the top actually require strong executive leadership from time to time; without it, they can become flustered and flounder. The group still needs the leader to take over periodically and maintain the "clearing in the forest."

5. It is unlikely that new leadership groups can quickly learn to work as a real team unless they already know each other well, have

worked in team modes before, and truly believe in the potential for team performance.

As this book went to press, Ben & Jerry's Homemade, Inc., was going through yet another CEO transition—in the face of increasingly severe market and performance pressures. Its current senior executives will face yet another period of adjustment to the style, priorities, and leadership approach of a new CEO. And, although the board of directors seems committed to maintaining at least some of the team performance capability that has developed among the top executives, it is impossible to predict how much of the team learning will carry forward with the new CEO. *True turnaround situations have precious little time for teams at any level.*

THE CAPABILITY TRADEOFF: POSITION VERSUS SKILL

To some extent, the sponsor (be it an executive or a group) of any potential team must consider the tradeoffs between the skills of the member candidates and their formal positions in the organization. Team discipline demands members with the right mix of skills (technical, problem-solving, and interpersonal) to accomplish the team's purpose; there is no compromise on that requirement. The team's acceptance by and ability to work effectively within the organization will, of course, also be affected by the positions of its members. In the pursuit of team performance, however, the position influence of the members must be a secondary consideration—or perhaps an additional one—after the multiple skill requirements have been met. In other words, *the formal position of the members cannot replace the working skill requirements.*

With teams at the top, the clear ranking of skills over position in picking team members is less clear for three reasons: (1) each top executive will likely possess a broad range of skills that appear to fit most of the performance issues and tasks that warrant teaming at the top; (2) position or influence over major portions of the organization can be as critical in resolving performance issues at the top as any specific functional or business skill; and (3) many skill deficiencies at the top can be filled with people from outside the team who can contribute on an as-needed basis. As a result, top leadership groups often make a reasonable decision when they give equal or higher priority to the formal position of the members for certain team issues. Nonetheless, they will still sacrifice real team levels of performance if needs for specific working skills are overlooked.

The problem, however, is not with occasional staffing decisions based on a conscious tradeoff of skill fit for position; it's with automatic or habitual decisions made without consciously considering the tradeoffs. When such representational staffing of team opportunities becomes mandatory, team performance suffers unless the skill requirements are somehow maintained. This is more likely to occur at the top than down the line. In most high-performing cultures, the mastery of team discipline down the line ensures that the required complementary skills will get the attention they deserve. This is less true at the top, where the carefree labeling of working groups as teams has also led to a habitual assignment of team performance tasks to organizational unit teams or working groups—with the assumption that job title equates with skill.

A significant part of the solution to the skill mismatch described above is obvious: expand the universe of possible candidates to include a rich enough pool to provide all the essential representational and skill needs in the candidates. Simple as it sounds, too many top leadership groups are blind to this option. For example, the top leadership group of a large multinational company was recently confronted with a virtual disaster in its management information systems (MIS) function. Years of inept leadership, misallocation of resources, and procrastination had produced an intolerable situation. When the team at the top finally acknowledged the magnitude of the MIS problem, it was on the critical path. Without a major transformation in the MIS function, there was little doubt that the company would lose its competitiveness and either go out of business or be acquired.

It seemed obvious to top management that they needed to hire an MIS miracle worker or retain outside consultants to reengineer the entire information systems function. The leadership group convened in several intensive sessions to evaluate its options and decide on a course of action. None of the group members had any MIS experience, yet they proceeded without changing the group composition. They simply assumed that the CFO would be able to provide the necessary

MIS knowledge and judgment. Without further ado, they concluded that the only answer was to retain outside consultants. Several bids later, they entered into a five-year, nearly $100 million contract to reengineer the function. Several months later, they had to bring in a "hired gun" executive to straighten out the mess, which by this time had virtually brought the institution to a standstill.

Who is to say that they might have resolved the issue differently if they had tapped into the MIS expertise within their own institution? Skeptics will argue that these were the people who created the mess, so they could hardly be counted on to decide how it should be cleaned up. On the other hand, the organization had a number of extremely skilled MIS professionals, who, despite their involvement in its creation, did know what the mess consisted of and realized that a consultant-intensive solution would meet more resistance than it could ever overcome. This is often the result of a prevailing mindset in top leadership groups. It presumes that the collective judgment and experience of those on the top team will somehow make up for its lack of more specific and relevant work skills.

Conversely, the team at the top of Ben & Jerry's went for the right set of skills. The emerging team had recruited Kathy Greenleaf, a top human resources executive, who had extensive experience and know-how in the people development area. Yet she also knew that there was a great deal about the Ben & Jerry's people situation that her skills could not handle. Against resistance from both her colleagues and board members, she held out for the assignment of operating managers to work with her on a team to redesign the company's management development process. There is no question that Greenleaf already knew how management development processes should work; what she did not know is what it would take for such processes to work within Ben & Jerry's. Note that there was also a "representation" element in her insistence on reaching out to the operating managers. In her mind, the representational "skill," or the credibility and influence that operating managers would have simply by virtue of their positions, was every bit as critical as management development skill. Moreover, she knew that she could not obtain the same credibility (and therefore the results she needed) in any other way.

The key considerations in making the tradeoff between position influence and skill mix have to do with the relative importance and difficulty of the skills necessary for the performance task. In some cases, it is reasonable to assume that the occupants of particular positions will have adequate skills for a particular team assignment. It is a mistake, however, not to give conscious consideration to the kind and level of skills required—both at the member level and in the group or team leader. Figure 6.2 positions a number of different kinds of potential teams with respect to the relative importance of the position (or influence) of the leader and the team members versus the importance of individual work skills relative to collective work skills. This positioning is illustrative only, as these situations can vary greatly depending on the particular kind of team or group. Nonetheless, in most functional department groups or teams, the influence of the leader in the organization is critical, whereas, with self-directed work teams, the influence of the leader is much less important than the

Figure 6.2
THE CAPABILITY TRADEOFF: *POSITION VERSUS SKILL*

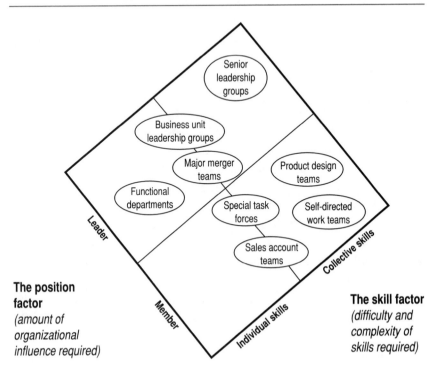

members' collective skills. It is worth noting, as Figure 6.2 indicates, that, for teams that run things (such as senior and business unit leadership groups), it is important to take account of both position and skill factors.

THE CAPACITY TRADEOFF: DIVERSITY VERSUS CLARITY

As pointed out earlier, there are three useful litmus tests for teams: *(1) the value of collective work products, (2) the mutual accountability of the members, and (3) a leadership role that shifts among the members.* This latter test is sometimes mistakenly viewed as the absence of leadership; hence, the commonly used labels of "self-directed" or "leaderless" teams. A real team is never leaderless, but it does have the capability of drawing on the leadership ability of each of its members at different times and in different ways.

A working group or organizational unit team is under the guidance and direction of its formal leader. Although he or she may opt to give a lead responsibility to one of the members on particular assignments, the formal leader is still accountable and all the members know it. Seldom does a member take an initiative that is not strongly endorsed, if not suggested, by the formal leader. The advantage of this approach lies in the clarity of leadership—it is always the same individual and in the clear line of individual accountability. This is a time-honored way for organizations to maintain order and accountability as they become larger over time.

Real teams, once they have become functional as teams, derive significant incremental leadership capacity from their ability to shift the leadership role back and forth among the members, depending on what the performance task requires. Admittedly, this cannot happen if their leader decides to prevent it, but *it does not necessarily require the leader to adopt a different style.* As will be described in the next chapter, Lou Noto's style at Mobil is dramatically different from Marc Shapiro's style at Texas Commerce Bank. Noto is outspoken, blunt, and frank, whereas Shapiro is thoughtful, quiet, and articulate. Yet both are able to derive significant leadership capacity from their executive group in team modes without changing their basic styles of leadership. Moreover, it isn't simply a matter of the formal leader (CEO) "wearing two hats," being assertive at times and stepping back at other times. The leadership role can shift only if one of the team members recognizes the need to exercise his initiative and all other members of the group welcome that initiative. The formal leader's "stepping back" is no more important in this interchange than the behaviors of each and every member of the group. In fact, formal leaders always benefit if they know they can assert themselves freely and be appropriately overridden by the rest of the team.

Pall Corporation, described in the preceding chapter, provides a good illustration of how the leadership role at the top can shift when a top leadership group is in a team mode. It also demonstrates the importance of the skill mix in both determining the team mode and establishing the leadership role. From the day that Maurice Hardy joined in the early 1960s, the leadership group at Pall Corporation shifted its priorities to establishing an international position in Europe. And, as indicated earlier, it was Hardy's special competence or skill (European know-how) that made this possible. Hence, it is not surprising that, for most issues that required Hardy's special competence, the leadership role within the top team shifted to him.

That did not, however, make him solely accountable for the company's European success or failure. It is clear in retrospect that Hardy could not have failed individually (only the team could have failed) and the team members all felt responsible and mutually accountable to one another. Although respective "areas of competence" mattered a lot, formal job boundaries did not seem to matter at all. Dr. Pall's role was clearly unique ("You can only have one genius," says Krasnoff) as the source of technological vision and capability. He was probably somewhat of a spiritual leader for the team. On the other hand, both Krasnoff and Hardy learned a lot about each other's disciplines (said Hardy, "I've taught Abe engineering, he's taught me accounting"), and both learned marketing out of sheer necessity. Asked if one of the team was thought of as "boss," Hardy says: "strange that you should ask that. I don't think so. At least, I've never detected it . . . we're all our own people . . . probably pretty unemployable in any normal company."

Perhaps the fact that they were such an oddball group worked to their advantage in shifting the leadership role as the occasion demanded. Each joined the team because of a unique set of work skills and leadership capabilities—not personality or style compatibility. The mixture of personalities, therefore, was actually an obstacle that they had to overcome whenever they needed to operate in a real team mode. Clearly, the importance of their purpose and their commitment to a global leadership vision made it natural for them to shift the leadership role to accomplish their goals.

No single member of the leadership group really functioned as the overall "boss." Rather, each became leader when the issue, situation, or problem to be resolved required his particular competence or perspective. No one ever hesitated to question the others, and each respected the inputs of the others even when those inputs lay outside their particular area of expertise.

The three senior leaders at Pall continued to function in a team mode even into their seventies. Obviously, the frequency became less as the active leadership of the company was distributed among many others and their roles changed. Their influence as a team, however, continues to be reflected in the company's strong performance ethic and deep commitment to values of competence and trust. In the beginning, it was easy for the leaders to operate in a team mode simply because of the company's venture attributes of small size, crystal-clear purpose (survival), and high level of commitment (their personal net worths were at stake).

As the company grew beyond a venture, however, the group took on additional members and found different team modes that worked. It also continued to violate some of the established beliefs and assumptions that inhibit the formation of teams at the top of more conventional corporate situations. The membership of their various team efforts was never hierarchically determined—it was determined by competence requirements. The style of the leader was not all-important, and no one worried about changing anyone else's leadership style for team purposes, because the group never really anointed a single leader. Even after Hardy became the official CEO, no one in the senior leadership group regarded him as the boss. When they were in a team mode, their purpose and approach were never "prescribed by the leader."

This tradeoff between clarity of leadership and additional leadership capacity is particularly important at the top, primarily because the top group often contains some of the most experienced and best leaders in the company. If that capability is not shared in team modes across critical corporate issues, it can represent a significant loss of leadership capacity. It may be that the capability of these top executives is better confined to their areas of primary responsibility. If so, however, that decision should be consciously made—not inadvertently the product of lack of awareness or skills for shifting into team modes and disciplines.

Different kinds of small groups can provide a different mix or balance with respect to leadership capacity versus leadership clarity. Obviously, the permanent single leader provides the most clarity, and the real team (whose leadership role shifts among the members) provides the most capacity.

CONCLUSION: CONSIDER ALL THE TRADEOFFS AND OPTIONS

The issue of team performance at the top rests with the options and the tradeoffs associated with them. Unless a top leadership group is willing and able to vary its mode of interaction and its membership configuration, it can function only as a working group. When crises strike, the team option comes more sharply into focus. Ben & Jerry's, however, is a good example of how difficult it can be for emerging leadership groups to draw on real team capability during a crisis. It is also an example of why it is so important for leadership groups to recognize the difference and develop—in advance—the ability to recognize when a real team is called for and when a strong single-leader group fits best.

I met with Jerry Junkins, the late CEO of Texas Instruments (TI), and his senior leadership group in early 1996. The purpose of that session was to explore options for strengthening their effectiveness as a team at the top. Much of what we discussed concerned the difference between the real team and single-leader modes, and the kinds of collective work products that would warrant application of team discipline. Like most top leadership groups that learn more about these options, they were somewhat relieved, because the session suggested to them that they might already be capitalizing on their team opportunities in subgroups. After the meeting, George Consolver, director of TI's strategy process, took me aside to express a major concern.

"You let them off the hook," he said pointedly. Consolver has years of experience with teams and with TI's senior leaders, so I did not take his comment lightly. In fact, he was articulating the biggest worry I have in working with senior leadership groups: that, when they understand the value of the single-leader working group option, they will back off of their desire for team performance at the top. The options work only if senior leaders are rigorous in their language, their choices between real team and single-leader modes, and their application of the appropriate discipline. Otherwise, Consolver was absolutely right!

Top leadership groups that use the language of teams while retaining the constraints of working groups not only suboptimize their performance contribution as a group, but confuse the rest of the organization. This latter problem is particularly troublesome in organizations that have both a strong performance ethic and a number of real teams in key places below the top. Thus it behooves top leadership groups to develop a better understanding of the options and tradeoffs that team performance implies, give serious consideration to the complete range available to them, and clean up their language accordingly. It may or may not make sense, after carefully considering the tradeoffs, for a particular leadership group to shift into a team mode more often—but it certainly will make sense to describe their efforts in words that do not confuse either themselves or the better team performers throughout the company.

CHAPTER SEVEN

Multiple Roles for the CEO

I USED TO BELIEVE that the CEO himself was the primary factor determining why we see so few real teams at the top. The essence of this argument is that, unless the CEO changes from an authoritative to a participative style, he cannot function as a team leader, and therefore no real team performance can be expected. I no longer hold this point of view. It turns out that, as long as the CEO truly believes in the power of team performance relative to other options and is willing to play a number of different roles, he need *not* change his style—nor need he be the team leader!

Role multiplicity is the name of this game. In 1996 Michael Keaton starred in an offbeat Hollywood movie called *Multiplicity*. Although the movie is a comedic fantasy, it makes a relevant point. The Keaton character, through a quirk of fate, is able to clone himself into several very different characters; however, each clone's personality and behavioral traits emphasize a particular attribute of the main character. For example, one clone is brash and masculine, one is sensitive and feminine, and one is childlike. Each capitalizes on its main attribute and set of accompanying traits to play very different roles in the Keaton character's life, and is thereby able to accomplish things that the others cannot.

Playing multiple roles is something that most executives do instinctively, particularly those who are sensitive to the needs of people around them. The best executives rely as much on their ability to judge, work with, and develop the better people in their organizations as they do on their strategic and economic capabilities. Thus, although they maintain a hierarchy that is focused on individual accountability, most learn to modify their role in that hierarchy to motivate and influence their people.

Daniel Goleman, in his book *Emotional Intelligence,* makes a compelling case for the importance of "emotional intelligence" (distinct from, but complementary to, the intelligence measured by traditional IQ tests) in successful people. Goleman's definition of emotional intelligence includes "abilities such as being able to motivate oneself and persist in the face of frustrations; to control impulse and delay gratification; to regulate one's moods and keep distress from swamping the ability to think; to empathize and to hope."[1] He argues that the better top leaders have learned to draw as much or more on their emotional maturity and their people sensitivity and skills than they do on their intellect and logic to influence people. As a result, they are able to play different roles within their formal position, to draw out potential contributions from others. Certainly, this is true for those top leaders—such as Dick Olson at Champion, Jim Rogers at GE, Bob Bauman at SmithKline, and Lou Noto at Mobil—who are able to extract from their top group both team performance (based on mutual accountability for collective work products) and individual executive performance (based on individual achievement and accountability). It is because of their unique balance of both intellect and emotional intelligence that they are able to perceive and play a variety of different roles in leading their companies, as well as obtain the performance potential from their top leadership group.

Strong leadership at the top—particularly by those who consistently lead their organizations to higher and higher levels of performance—is the hallmark of every successful company. Periodically, quality business publications identify and profile the best chief executives, either in feature articles or sometimes in so-called lists of the best. These profiles invariably focus on the superior intellect, wisdom, and discipline of such leaders—in other words, on the qualities reflected in the executive leadership discipline described in earlier chapters. Unfortunately, as already illustrated, executive leadership discipline often crowds out team performance discipline.

Perhaps the most disciplined and tough-minded CEOs are the turnaround heroes—those who bravely enter the dark chasms of a faltering or failing enterprise and somehow snatch victory from the jaws of defeat. Such miracle workers command high rewards for their efforts, as well as the admiration of those of us who can but marvel at their ability to cut through to the heart of the problem, make the tough decisions to prune assets and overheads, and restructure the entire organization into a leaner, meaner, and more responsive company. They appear relentlessly disciplined about what it takes to transform a loser into a winner; however, seldom does that discipline include the basic elements of team discipline. The turnaround leader does not have much time to worry about teams.

To the casual observer, therefore, the turnaround leader, as well as the CEOs of high-performing companies, are anything but natural team leaders. They may pay lip service to their "top team," but it is not a real team. Certainly, they are meticulous about selecting individual executives who can take individual responsibility for particular issues or situations, deliver against demanding assignments, and stand up to the pressure of relentless individual accountability for results. But, when all is said and done, these so-called teams at the top function primarily as strong, single-leader working groups and rely on organization unit teams within the hierarchy.

A number of very effective CEOs simply do not (or cannot) function as real team leaders themselves—because of their own attitudes, beliefs, and strong personal preferences, or because of the expectations of their people, or both. For example, it is difficult to picture executives like Charles Knight of Emerson Electric, John Welch of General Electric, or William Gates of Microsoft functioning in a real team leader role—even though each undoubtedly encourages real team efforts in his organization. On the other hand, it isn't so hard to picture Lewis Platt of Hewlett-Packard or Robert Haas of Levi Strauss functioning as team leaders.

The point is *not* that one approach is necessarily better than the other; all of these CEOs lead high-performing companies that benefit from real teams in a number of critical areas. The point is that, with either approach, I contend there is an opportunity to be more discriminating and rigorous about when and where to apply team discipline among the senior leadership group. The following sections draw in more detail on two situations from earlier chapters to illustrate how different CEO styles and roles can affect the balance between team and nonteam efforts at the top. In the first case, Andrew Sigler at Champion did not function as a team leader, whereas in the second case, Lucio Noto at Mobil did. And both were able to obtain a better balance of team performance at the top.

LEADERSHIP ROLES AT CHAMPION

Chapter 1 describes how Andrew Sigler provided the visionary, strategic, and tough decision-making leadership that took Champion through ten years of very difficult cultural and performance change within the paper mills. His early vision of "investing in superior paper-making machines and team-based people systems" required a strong will and the courage to resist the persistent attacks of nonbelievers, both inside and outside of the company. In addition, his individual leadership over time kept the organization focused, aligned, and energized during many difficult periods. To most observers, be they critics or supporters, Sigler was a classic model of a strong-willed, decisive CEO—not a team leader.

Nonetheless, under Sigler's leadership Champion became one of the early pioneers in the development of self-directed work team approaches at the mill level, not only within its industry, but also across the broad industrial sector of North America. And, as a result of these efforts, the company's operating performance improved markedly, and many of its mills today are among the best performers in the industry.

The Senior Leadership Group

At the top of the company, however, Sigler's direct reports remained basically a single-leader working group for nearly ten years. As we have already seen, although they seriously explored the possibility of functioning as a team, it was clear to all that the conditions that favored real teams elsewhere in the company were not present at the top. For one thing, it was difficult to identify either a clear group purpose or a set of high-value, collective work products that would coalesce a team encompassing the entire group. More importantly, perhaps, Sigler did little to encourage any shifting of the top leadership role. He was never one to step back and let someone else lead in a direction with which he was uncomfortable—nor was he reluctant to let others know when he was uncomfortable. As a result, people throughout the organization came to expect, as well as to draw comfort from, his strong individual leadership.

Yet, despite the fact that he did not function as a team leader himself, he filled a number of team-supportive roles and produced an impressive blend of team and working group performance throughout the company. Perhaps the most important of these was his highly visible role of carrying the "team performance banner" at all times. Because of the years of testing, trying, and shaping team approaches in the mills, Sigler was a true believer in team performance. There was no doubt in his mind that real teams significantly outperform working groups when the market, competitive, and workplace conditions call for team performance. Nor was there any doubt in the minds of his management group of his conviction with regard to teams.

Above all, however, he was a realist who had no illusions about his own ability to play a team leader role within his corporate leadership group. His long established patterns of interaction with his executives were too firmly ingrained to permit Sigler to play any real team leader role. So he simply looked for opportunities to enable others to lead team efforts whenever he believed an executive team mode was appropriate. His experience in shaping team approaches within the paper mills became of increasing value to him as that experience expanded. It enabled him to think easily in terms of multiple teams, subteams, and working groups without worrying about either terminology or appearances—whatever configuration was required to get the job done, although he usually gave the team option careful consideration to be sure he wasn't missing the performance potential that real teams represent. But nobody knew better than Sigler that trying for teams everywhere is utter nonsense.

At the same time, he believed strongly that the leadership group as a group not only needed to be sustained for the next CEO to succeed, it also needed to be able to function as a real team when appropriate. The Champion organization and working environment are not easily understood nor wisely put into the hands of an outsider. Hence, Sigler designed the leadership transition process described earlier (Chapter 1) whereby the senior group of 18 executives met together and in subteams over a two-year period to identify and address the key strategic, performance, and people development issues facing the company going forward. In these sessions, Sigler remained the clear leader, and the group functioned primarily as a working group.

As they identified issues and opportunities with team potential, however, Sigler would play a number of different roles. First, he was insistent that group members force their thinking with respect to each issue's relative importance to the future performance of the enterprise. Second, he was influential in how the issues were framed with respect to practicality and performance impact. And he was alert to any potential team opportunity and, therefore, to how it was scoped and staffed. For example, when they began to engage around corporate strategy (an area that Sigler and Heist had handled themselves in the past), he guided the selection of a team that included most of the likely successor candidates. However, he set it up in such a way as to virtually neutralize any succession or hierarchical politics. In fact, the "junior" member of the group was the designated team leader (Mark Childers).

Often in the discussions, Sigler would allow, even encourage, conflicting points of view. But, when sensible resolution by the group became unlikely, he would intercede and lead the group to an integrative resolution, making sure to get the best of all viewpoints. With Sigler present, the discussions were certainly different than when he was absent, but the group was not particularly inhibited. He played multiple roles, including team disciplinarian, value enforcer, strategic educator, political diffuser, executive skill builder, and decision maker—to name a few. In all cases, however, he had one overriding purpose: to enable the group to develop its individual and collective capabilities to assume the leadership of the company upon his retirement. To be sure, he was also evaluating the options for his successor, but that was truly secondary to his executive development purpose.

The Emerging New Team at the Top

In fact, the final choice for the next CEO really was not the most important succession issue in Sigler's mind. His primary concern was the shaping of a collective unit or potential team to succeed him. He believed that, if the senior leadership group could build cohesiveness and capitalize on its ability to function in a team mode, no single CEO choice was imperative. Throughout this two-year process, a number of real team efforts evolved, as did many successful single-leader working groups. As we saw in Chapter 1, the new CEO, Richard Olson, is shaping his own leadership approach, already quite different from Sigler's. Significantly, Olson is a more natural team leader and often functions in that role, whereas Sigler did not. Thus it will be surprising indeed if he does not place a higher emphasis on integrating team and executive leadership disciplines and performance at the top. If so, Sigler's hopes for a more cohesive and adaptable team at the top may become a reality.

Of course, the senior leaders will fill complementary but different roles in leading the company than was the case under Sigler. And the roles that Olson assumes are not the same as those played by Sigler. For example, both of the two most senior leaders, Olson and Nichols, can lead as well as participate as members of team efforts at the top. In addition, Olson is an excellent one-on-one counselor for other team members. He often helps them understand how to modify their individual behavior patterns and attitudes to enable better team performance. Obviously, Olson's style as CEO is completely different from Sigler's. Both are able to play a variety of roles consistent with their individual styles, which enables real team efforts, but Olson's will clearly lead to more team performance at the top.

The Champion story illustrates a number of critical points about the roles that senior leaders can play to improve the balance between team and nonteam performance within their senior leadership groups, most notably:

■ The CEO need not be a team leader as long as he or she can play multiple support roles that enable subteam efforts and enforce the essential discipline of teams with respect to those efforts.

■ It is important for the senior leadership group to understand and recognize the difference between situations that call for team discipline and those that require single-leader discipline.

■ It helps a great deal if the group has had firsthand experience with real team performance elsewhere in the organization and are believers in its potential at the top.

SENIOR ROLE CHANGES AT MOBIL CORPORATION

Lucio Noto, CEO of Mobil, is another good example of how the better CEOs can play a multiplicity of roles—without changing their basic leadership style—to obtain a balance of team and nonteam performance within their top leadership groups. The first discussion I recall with Noto on this topic was when he and Rex Adams, his top "people advisor" and human resources executive, were exploring the possibility of shaping a team out of an executive committee of seven executives. It was not the most propitious of times, nor did it grow out of the most natural team environment.

Historical Perspective

As in most major oil companies, the formal hierarchical structure of the organization had been the dominant method for aligning behaviors and decisions across a large, complex, and increasingly global enterprise. Although not exactly militaristic, the emphasis had clearly been on formal roles and individual accountability; team efforts at the top had been few and far between. Several generations of CEOs preceding Noto had run their organizations very successfully with a strong, one-on-one approach supplemented by single-leader working groups and hierarchical organization unit teams.

Noto's immediate predecessor was Allen Murray. During Murray's tenure as CEO, the company restructured its corporate center, moving it from New York to Fairfax, Virginia. Although some team efforts may have emerged during this period, virtually none of them were evident among the leadership group at Fairfax. Murray's interactions with his executives were primarily one-on-one discussions, and the group sessions for formal meetings were tightly held to predetermined agendas with no surprises. It was an efficient hierarchical leadership approach, but it produced almost no real team performance at the top, even when major issues or opportunities might have warranted a team approach.

Rex Adams can recall only one or two times when a small group of the top executives operated in a team mode for short periods of time—but the CEO was neither the instigator of nor an active participant in those efforts. They came about because of an urgent situation that was handled informally. This same pattern of behavior had been true under the preceding leadership of Rawleigh Warner, Jr., and William Tavoulareas. Although it might be said that they ran the company as a two-person team, in truth each followed his own rigorous executive leadership discipline within clearly understood areas of responsibility.

Warner dealt with external leadership matters, and Tavoulareas ran the businesses—again in a one-on-one context with efficient single-leader working group interactions when group alignments were required.

Noto's "Dream Team"

Despite the long history of organization unit leadership at Mobil, Noto believed it was time to try for team performance at the top. Although surprising to some, his view was understandable. Noto had been an unexpected choice as CEO because the selection leaped over the normal organizational and seniority patterns of the past. At least three other executives were senior to him and had substantially more operating experience, individually and certainly collectively. Moreover, they were seasoned executives with strong performance and people development accomplishments in their records. Noto himself claims he was a reluctant winner of the CEO prize, as he expected one of the others to be chosen and it was not a job to which he particularly aspired.

It was natural, therefore, that he would seek to shape a strong teamlike contingent around him, both to capitalize on the experience and capabilities of the senior executives and to reach for the higher performance results that real teams can achieve. He also believed strongly that Mobil was at a critical juncture in its development. The industry was undergoing significant changes, competitors were modifying both strategies and structures, and growth prospects were becoming more difficult to identify and realize. In short, he needed all the senior help he could get, and he needed that group to be "in the boat" with him in positioning Mobil to strengthen its strategic position and leadership capacity for the next generation of management.

So why not a team at the top? Adams was even more skeptical than I was and, as always, bluntly on target about how hard it would be for this group to function as a team. Not only was it contrary to the historic leadership patterns of the past, but none of the current group had operated in a real team mode for many years. Their personal favorite approach was based on traditional executive leadership disciplines, at which all of them excelled and which had worked very well for them. Why should they change now? Of equal concern was the not-so-friendly competition and the occasional lack of trust among some members of the group. This created a group dynamic that was hardly conducive to anything but discussion, debate, and communication. Collective work products, joint accountability, and shared leadership were never part of that dynamic and unlikely to become so easily.

The Staff Redesign Project

Noto, however, had more confidence in his senior group working as a team than either Adams or I realized. Moreover, he had just endorsed the work of the Staff Redesign Project (SRP), a special, multiteam effort led by Robert Swanson and Rex Adams of the senior leadership group. Its purpose was to increase the overall effectiveness of staff services, particularly those emanating from the corporate center in Fairfax, Virginia. The consulting firm of Booz, Allen and Hamilton provided valuable outside consulting support, and the effort succeeded in streamlining staff services and saving millions of dollars. The recommendations included significant redesign of many staff functions and a different view of senior executive leadership roles. This redesign would, in effect, leave most of the senior leadership group without the same executive responsibilities as before. In short, the part of their jobs requiring the executive leadership discipline that they were masters at was being deemphasized—and it was not clear what would replace it. Skeptical observers argued that the senior leadership group was becoming superfluous.

Noto knew better. These were the most experienced, able executives in the company, and he needed them now more than ever. If their former line executive roles were no more, then he was determined to shape different ones and was prepared to play a number of different roles himself to make that happen. Somewhat fortuitously, the Staff Redesign Project provided the starting point. Its recommendations resulted in a difficult people placement situation, as the corporate staff restructuring resulted in nearly 75 legitimate candidates for only 25 positions. A special group of top managers (one level below the executive committee) was assigned to evaluate and recommend people for those positions. It was a difficult, serious, and compelling task, and the group set about it with a high level of common commitment to "get the right person in the right job" based on performance, skills, and potential—not position, politics, or tenure.

A "Forerunner" Team Shows the Way

The challenge cried out for team performance, and, not too surprisingly, this "cross-functional committee," as they were called, rose to the occasion. Their efforts not only resolved the staffing of the 25 jobs, they also introduced a powerful new approach for the development of leadership talent in the future. Noto and his executive committee immediately saw this broader opportunity. If they could develop a more rigorous and effective process of evaluating and developing their best people, it could extend well beyond the immediate task of picking the best 25 for the new staff jobs. Their ad hoc team had inadvertently found a way to resolve the company's most critical performance need going forward: the accelerated development of global leadership capacity. Assuming that the ad hoc team could impart the principles and approach used in this one-time, critical staffing situation to a similarly structured process, it should be possible to accelerate the development of leadership capacity on a much broader scale.

Thus emerged the first credible "team challenge" for the new senior leadership group: create a new process for accelerating the development of leadership capacity, and determine how to extend and implement the new approach across all key parts of the company. The solution turned out to be a balanced combination of team and working group forums interacting with what would become the newly constituted Executive Office (EO), functioning in a real team mode, as an integral part of the new process.

New Roles for EO Members

Both Noto and his senior leadership group found themselves playing a number of different roles throughout the design, testing, and implementation of the new process. In effect, the Staff Redesign Project had opened the way for trying, testing, and shaping a more flexible senior leadership group (the Executive Office). In the beginning, Noto had to take a strong, individual leadership role because of the reluctance, if not resistance, among some of his senior leaders to the potential changes in their previous strong executive responsibilities. A lack of common commitment at that point made any real team effort among the top group difficult. In the selection of the "cross-functional committee," however, the senior leadership group worked well together, approaching that of a real team. Noto played a much different role in those sessions, because the common level of commitment to get the right team working on this sensitive situation was strong enough for others to lead when their people were being considered.

The cross-functional committee returned with a recommendation that the Executive Office members follow a new approach in evaluating candidates' performance and potential for compensation and advancement purposes. Each member of the EO (including Noto) was required to conduct extensive interviews and review a new base of performance facts on a set of individuals with whom they had not worked recently. This was a different kind of real work role for the members. Moreover, once each had developed the information base required with respect to their assigned candidates, the group had to come together and work in a team mode to complete the evaluation of the candidates. Noto functioned as both a team member and a team leader—but seldom as CEO—in these efforts. The same can be said of the other members of the senior leadership group.

Yet, while the executives functioned in a variety of different roles throughout this process, none of them really changed his basic leadership style. Noto remained outspoken, frank, and decisive, as well as being a very careful listener; Paul Hoenmans was organized, thoughtful, precise, and determined; Renna was open, insightful, blunt, and constructively confrontational; Swanson was the wise integrator of differing views; Adams was the consummate "devil's advocate" and kept the rest of the group honest. Each played different roles within these fundamental personal styles—and it worked very well. Their high level of commitment to do right by the next generation of leadership was evident to all and resulted in an increasingly strong level of trust building within the group. To outsiders, they still looked very much like a nonteam, but behind closed doors they functioned in a powerful team mode.

Noto's multiple roles came about primarily as a result of his "filling the gaps" whenever the group's progress seemed to falter. His strong belief in both the capability and the experience of each individual member, as well as his conviction about their team potential, served him well. Because of those beliefs, it was possible for him to take chances with the group in a nonleader role, to enforce the discipline of both executive leadership and team basics, and to actually neutralize the politics of the hierarchy, which occasionally got in the way. He was diligent in subtly reminding the group of the main theme of their effort—to accelerate the development of the next generation of Mobil's top leadership group. He was particularly effective at integrating the conflicting points of view without either compromising valid ideas or inserting his own viewpoint too forcefully. Most of all, he succeeded in virtually destroying the natural pecking order within the group.

These are not "roles" in the formal, organizational sense of the word. Nor have I described all the different roles that various team members played. Hopefully, however, the multiplicity of required roles is evident—as are their wide-ranging characteristics. Although there are a number of useful lessons to be learned from this example, three in particular are worth reemphasizing:

1. Even the most senior line executives can function in a team mode if the need is clear, the purpose is compelling, and the CEO plays a subordinate role from time to time.

2. People development issues are natural rallying points for senior executive team efforts, largely because they are consistent with the best executives' strong belief in the value of developing their people.

3. Senior executives need not change their basic leadership style, although they do need to be willing to try different roles and working approaches. They also need to be able to shift back into their single-leader roles.

As this example indicated, Noto's personal style and leadership philosophy were very different from those of his predecessors at Mobil, particularly with respect to how he chose to capitalize on the leadership capacity of his upper management people. The following example from the Texas Commerce Bank further illustrates how different successful leadership styles affect team performance at the top.

TEXAS COMMERCE BANK

The Texas Commerce Bank (TCB) no longer stands alone. In 1987 it became part of Chemical Bank of New York, and in 1996 Chemical and Chase merged to form the largest bank in North America. These absorptions, however, cannot obscure the outstanding performance record of TCB between 1960 and the present. To be sure, there have been ups and downs—no one really weathered the banking crises of the 1980s without suffering—but TCB continues as one of the best regional banking institutions in the country. Its history is marked by two excellent CEOs, whose styles could not be more different.

Historical Perspective

Marc Shapiro is the current CEO of Texas Commerce Bank. He is a product and an ardent admirer of his mentor and predecessor, Ben Love. Yet they are as different as night and day in their leadership styles and approaches. Both, however, were very successful. Love's remarkable leadership during the over 20 years of building TCB into the number one regional bank in the country is a matter of record. And he is still a respected and committed leader in the Houston business community, where he resides. He epitomizes the image of the ideal CEO which I developed during my formative years at the Harvard Business School—a clear visionary, with strong personal and business values of integrity, high standards of leadership that focus on quality service, customer-responsive employees, and shareholder value. He also placed the highest premium on getting the very best people, particularly among his management ranks. Some would consider him an elitist in his relentless pursuit of the best talent he could attract. When my firm was trying to establish a position in Texas, Love was invariably our toughest competitor for top people.

Love set demanding performance standards for himself as well as his executives, and he expected those standards to be met. He believed in delegating authority and responsibility to those who earned that right and in holding them individually accountable. His basic leadership approach was one-on-one interaction with his top executives, supplemented by group sessions that were open, efficient single-leader working groups. When teams emerged to match compelling, unexpected performance challenges, Love was their sponsor and supporter, but not a member or team leader. Like Andrew Sigler at Champion, he recognized that team performance, on those rare occasions when it was needed, was more likely to occur if he played a sponsor role rather than that of a team leader. In his classic CEO style, Love played a number of different roles, but most of them were focused on leveraging the individual talent and potential of this superior pool of managers. They are not, however, roles that enable team performance except insofar as they produce demanding and compelling performance challenges that can be achieved only in a team mode.

Shapiro developed as an executive working within Love's approach. He gained a deep appreciation for the kind of leadership roles in which Ben excelled and learned well the elements of executive leadership discipline. He observed Love playing the kinds of roles that inspired respect and performance from individuals, and he didn't forget how to play those roles. He later learned the elements of small-group performance and team discipline on the job as CEO—largely because the marketplace situation changed, and the need for team performance became much more urgent than it had been in earlier years.

Whereas Love publicly emphasized the traditions of the bank and the fact that it was a great institution, Shapiro puts more emphasis on the great people he believes make up the enterprise. He also has a more natural desire to be accessible to people at all levels. When he took over as president, he moved the executive floor from the sixty-first floor to the second level, near the front lobby of an operating branch. No receptionist shields him from the public or from lower-level employees, which makes it much easier for him to be an active participant in and catalyst for the teamwork and customer service elements of his organization.

Process Improvement at TCB

The first major eye-opener for Shapiro with respect to real team performance came during a reengineering effort, which was called Process Improvement (PI) largely because of the negative image connected with the term *reengineering*. Shapiro had actually commissioned this effort in a straightforward attempt to take $50 million out of the cost base of the bank. His analysis had convinced him that accomplishment would return the bank to the top quartile of the regional banks with which TCB benchmarked itself. He established the goal and selected several task forces to determine how to reach it. In his mind, these were task forces similar to those that had worked successfully before in a customer service initiative, as well as in other efforts requiring resource application outside the normal organizational structure. They were invariably single-leader working groups, however, with the leaders being chosen because of their experience, stature, and skills in this kind of effort. Although he thought of them as teams, the mode of actual operation would have depended heavily on the leaders.

The PI task forces, however, not only made a change in the approach to this important program, but eventually their efforts led to a change in Shapiro's leadership approach. Task force members convinced him that the effort, to be successful at TCB, had to be focused on something much more meaningful to the workforce than cost reduction, as important as that might in fact be. Shapiro and his task force leaders conceived of an aspiration to "eliminate that which frustrates our customers and our bankers"—a small difference in focus, perhaps, but a huge difference in the way people throughout the bank would feel about the effort. And the way it came about was an important step in introducing a number of new roles into Shapiro's leadership approach.

Admittedly, his basic style was team-friendly to begin with—and Shapiro believes that style can make the difference. He is a very accessible, soft-spoken, attentive listener who appears to have little need for credit or public attention. As the PI process unfolded, not only did the task forces leading the effort begin shifting into team modes frequently and easily, but the entire effort expanded to involve close to half of the bank's 9,000 people in over 175 "action teams"—a great many of which worked consistently in a real team mode. As Shapiro and his leadership group saw this effort building momentum, they began to play roles that would further enable and encourage team performance at all levels.

Shapiro found himself spending close to half of his time interacting with the task forces and teams, with little or no regard for the hierarchical implications. He was a frequent attendee of both task force and action team meetings, where he observed, listened, and responded. He became a strong advocate of the action teams and worked with his people to make sure that both the skills and the goals were clear and appropriate, and produced mutual as well as individual account-ability. His top group was encouraged to work in team modes both among themselves and in conjunction with key groupings in the pro-cess down the line.

An interesting situation with a bank team illustrates Shapiro's role flexibility. The Customer side of the bank could not resolve a dispute with Operations over a critical customer service. TCB's approach to the service had been slow, with higher customer fees than charged by competitors. The Customer side had little reason to favor adding some of the operational enhancements found at other banks because its profitability would suffer. The departmental leaders could not re-solve the issues between themselves.

When Shapiro heard about the issues between the two departments in August 1995, he appointed a cross-organization team to resolve them. The team included members of TCB's internal consulting staff group and people at all levels of both departments. The team did a lot of work to learn about competitive actions and options, but by March 1996 no recommendations had emerged.

After three more months, Shapiro joined the group, first in a senior facilitator role, but then shifting into more of a working team member role. His ability to shift roles was very effective in breaking the logjam. In the course of the effort, he provided formal authority, acted as an impartial arbitrator, and helped in the problem solving without dictat-ing the answer. Not many CEOs exhibit that kind of role flexibility when working with leadership groups below the top.

In many situations with his senior leadership group, Shapiro oper-ates as an executive leader or in a single-leader working group mode. In others, particularly when the group involves managers outside the senior leader group, he functions more as a Socratic questioner and occasional team member. More often than not, however, he plays the critical role of team sponsor, team enabler, and performance challenger. Perhaps his most critical role in terms of increasing the team perform-ance capabilities in the bank is that of identifying the most important team opportunities and ensuring the right mix of skills and experience in the team members. These are roles and behavior patterns that were much less apparent with the previous CEO. Clearly, the style differences between the two leaders help explain the different balance between team and executive leadership performance, but I believe it is more than leadership style. It is a combination of very different marketplace conditions, which demand more team performance, and of Shapiro's growing awareness of the different role options he has for ensuring team performance when it is needed.

ROLE OPTIONS

Depending on the CEO's style, which is unlikely to change, the roles he or she plays will differ. And often he or she will get other members of the leadership group into some of the roles that fit his or her style less well. The following seven roles, which can be filled by most top executives who believe in the performance potential of real teams, can change the balance within any top leadership group. The questions following the description of each role are intended to focus the reader's attention on specifics that can help make the role more successful.

1. *Team opportunity spotter.* This role is basically that of identifying the most critical team opportunities and ensuring that the leadership group focuses attention on making them happen. Simply put, determine where obtaining real team performance matters most. Several of Marc Shapiro's key leaders view this as one of Shapiro's most important roles in building team performance at Texas Commerce Bank. The informal discussions of the leadership group at Ben & Jerry's, described earlier, identified over 40 different high-priority issues, problems, and opportunities. The big breakthrough for them, however, came in their subsequent deliberations, when they learned to distinguish the real team opportunities from the others and to prioritize those opportunities.

   Can you identify the half-dozen or so places where real teams would significantly improve performance results? If not, you may be overlooking an important weapon in your competitive arsenal.

2. *Monitor of team discipline.* This role is that of enforcing the discipline of teams to ensure that the performance benefits occur. The enforcement of the discipline is critical. Without it, the more in-

grained discipline of executive leadership will dominate and force out team behaviors. Because the two disciplines are often in conflict, the discipline of teams needs some help to survive against its stronger compatriot. The original leadership group at Pall Corporation knew instinctively that the international situation required a team discipline, whereas many of their domestic issues did not. Maurice Hardy was the primary enforcer of this discipline.

Do you understand the application of the five elements of team discipline discussed in Appendix B? If so, do you also make sure that the discipline is being applied in those situations that constitute your most important real team opportunities?

3. *Political neutralizer.* Unless someone actively neutralizes the politics of the hierarchy, team performance is unlikely. Although teams are not without their own simple hierarchy, it seldom follows the permanent hierarchy of the formal organization. Someone needs to play the role of neutralizing the formal hierarchy within team situations. Otherwise, the essential skill mix and leadership shifts required for real team performance will suffer. Project Delta at Citicorp occurred in the midst of the leadership transition from Wriston to Reed, and the politics of that situation prevented a real team from emerging. Conversely, Andrew Sigler was a master of grouping his leaders in ways that made the politics of succession less relevant and disturbing to the group's collective efforts.

Do you think consciously about the legitimate ambitions of your senior leadership group and take steps to group them in ways that minimize the politics within any group that needs to function as a real team?

4. *Theme and initiative shaper.* It is extremely valuable to concentrate the group's team efforts around a few key themes. The demands on any top leadership group are extensive and cover a wide range of activities, only some of which warrant the group's functioning in a team mode. The framing of a simple theme or initiative can often help pull an important team opportunity out of the maze of nonteam activity than engulfs executive agendas. Robert Bauman and his top teams at SmithKline Beecham were masters at crafting short, meaningful themes that helped focus and concentrate the efforts of many people. The senior leaders at Mobil initially

resisted the notion of themes as being too impractical, but as they became more comfortable in their new roles, they came to see that the themes of operating performance and leadership development would focus and energize their efforts as a group, as well as clarify for the rest of the organization what their priorities were.

Do you look for meaningful themes that can keep both team and single-leader working group efforts focused on the most critical priorities? Do you take advantage of the ideas and working experiences of others in shaping those themes?

5. ***Conflict integrator.*** Integrating conflicting points of view without compromise is a uniquely valuable skill. Top executive positions and performance discipline often lead to conflict and compromise rather than to integration. Richard Olson at Champion and Marc Shapiro at TCB each approached this role very differently, but both were able to achieve the kind of integration their situations required. As Mary Parker Follett reminded us earlier, true integration is far better than compromise or domination of a single viewpoint because "a solution has been found in which both [points of view] have found a place."[2] The integrator role is of vital importance in any top leadership group that aspires to achieve both high individual and team levels of performance.

Do you encourage constructive conflict in the working sessions of your senior leadership group? Do you allot enough time for these conflicts to result in the actual integration of the best ideas of all sides—or do you settle for an early compromise?

6. ***Skill mix monitor.*** All too often, a real team opportunity is missed because the members are assigned on the basis of their position in the company rather than their skills relative to the task at hand. A CEO who is alert to this risk can play an invaluable role in matching the skills to the performance need, particularly when those skills do not reside in the formal top leadership group. Lou Noto and Gene Renna at Mobil both play this role well as they lead the implementation of their new organization approach. Robert Holland realized this at Ben & Jerry's, but it was not until members of his emerging leadership group experienced the gap themselves that a common sense of urgency took hold, and they were able to add the skills required to fit the performance task.

Do you assign executives to subgroups based on position and job title rather than on actual skill mix relative to the task? Do you look outside the senior group to obtain the right skills on any important team opportunity?

7. *"Pecking order killer."* Teams have to do real work together if they are to produce the collective work products that are required for them to achieve their performance purpose. The formal or natural pecking order of their permanent jobs often works against this requirement. A CEO who is willing to step in and break up counterproductive pecking order behaviors will greatly enhance the team potential of his group. Lou Noto at Mobil is particularly effective in breaking up the pecking order instincts in his senior leadership group simply by the way he behaves himself. He will often position others in the lead role and function as a team member in a way that makes it clear that he doesn't consider his viewpoint to be any more important than anyone else's.

Do you behave in ways that break down the natural pecking order, by picking junior people to lead in both team and single-leader working group situations? Do you often turn the leadership role over to others within the senior leadership group?

Obviously, these seven roles are not the only ones that CEOs and top leaders can play to enhance team performance. I believe they are illustrative, however, of the kinds of roles and the range of different roles that are required in a balanced leadership approach that takes full advantage of the team performance potential at the top.

CONCLUSION: ROLES MATTER, NOT STYLE

CEOs do make the difference in the balance between team and non-team performance at the top. They set the tone, provide the leadership philosophy, and pick the leadership group with which they will work. That is as it should be. They cannot, however, mandate team performance at the top, and most certainly, their leadership style—whatever it may be—need not deter team performance. Sigler's style, for example, was truly intimidating to those who were not used to it; Shapiro's unassuming attitude was quite the opposite. Both, however, really believe in the potential upside of team performance, understand the discipline required, and learned to play different roles to apply that discipline. As a result, both were able to increase the amount of real team performance within their leadership groups.

The best CEOs have a clear leadership philosophy that serves them well. It fits their beliefs, skills, and experience. It invariably shapes their leadership style and determines the composition and attributes of their top leadership group. As we have seen, many different kinds of CEOs obtain team performance from their leadership groups when unexpected, demanding performance issues and opportunities arise. Because of the strong executive leadership discipline that permeates most successful top leadership groups, however, it takes a uniquely compelling performance situation for teams to emerge. As leadership groups experience the results of team performance in these situations, however, they can develop a conviction about its value that allows some to balance their executive leadership discipline with a team performance discipline. This requires the CEO, as well as each member of the senior leadership group, to play a variety of different roles than they might have played before.

For example, Figure 7.1 illustrates how the relative importance of collective work products and a leader's task know-how relative to the rest of the group should affect the leadership approach for any small-group challenge. As the relative importance of the collective work products increases relative to individual work products, it becomes more important for the leader of the group to function as a real team leader, allowing the actual leadership of the group to shift to the appropriate member or members, based on the task at hand. Similarly, as the actual task know-how of the various members of the team exceeds the know-how of the designated group leader, it becomes more important for that leader to shift the group into a real team approach.

Figure 7.1
LEADERSHIP APPROACHES

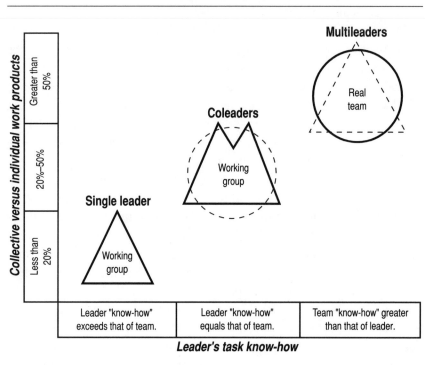

CHAPTER EIGHT

For "Teams That Run Things" at Any Level

"**I**T ALL REALLY STARTED with the window-jumping sessions," Richard Schaar said. Window jumping, I thought incredulously. Was he joking? No, it turns out that Schaar, Tom Ferrio, Tammy Richards, C. B. Wilson, and David Robin had an extended series of late Friday afternoon working sessions starting in 1986 that were christened "window-jumping" meetings. Apparently, in one of the early ones, someone pointed out that things were so bad that the best thing to do might be to simply jump out of the window. It was a joke, of course, but it had a perverse meaning that made the label stick.

This is a story about a team that started out nowhere near the top of anything—except perhaps the building out of whose window they were threatening to jump. It is also a remarkable success story of how the leaders of a stepchild calculator business within Texas Instruments somehow created a winner out of what appeared to be a losing situation. I first learned about it in an informal discussion about teams at the top, with Tom Engibous, CEO of Texas Instruments (TI). He was making a passing observation about one of his better performing units. "When it comes to top team accomplishments, I think of Richard Schaar's group. Perhaps a little stranger than most, but they have really turned the calculator business into a winner." Why, I wondered, did the notion of "team at the top" bring to mind a group in the middle? And what did their "strangeness" have to do with their performance? So I asked Engibous if he would mind my meeting with Schaar to learn more about this anomalous team at the top—in the middle.

"It's OK with me if it's OK with Richard. Just don't tell him I suggested it," he said, reflecting the strong norm within TI of leaving responsible managers to run their own operations without undue interference from above. So I arranged to meet with Schaar and learn more about his window-jumping group. As Engibous had described the remarkable accomplishments of Schaar's group, it was clear that some kind of top team behaviors were at work, although I was still pretty skeptical that it would be relevant for teams at the very top. Nonetheless, it was hard to ignore this group. They had succeeded in taking the calculator business from a negative return on a $100 million business to something approaching 30 percent return on net assets at close to five times the volume in less than ten years. Not only is this a unique "virtual venture" success within a large corporation, it also appeared to be a somewhat countercultural leadership approach within TI.

Schaar did not fit my image of a turnaround business leader. In fact, he looks much more like the distinguished, applied mathematics professor that he once was at the University of South Carolina (USC), with neatly trimmed graying hair and mustache framing a friendly, earnest face. His unassuming, soft-spoken manner belies a sharp mind, aggressive leadership approach, and articulate communication. I was also somewhat surprised to learn how familiar he was with the real world of teams and of his intense interest in learning more about obtaining team performance at TI.

It was clear that he was more than a bit concerned about the difficulties of sustaining real team performance in his group as it continues to grow in size and complexity. Things were a lot simpler when the group could contemplate jumping or not jumping out of windows.

WINDOW JUMPING AND BEYOND

The window-jumping sessions were more than a symbolic reminder of the potential team efforts. Every Friday afternoon for several years, this team came together to figure out how to run their calculator business—which was anything but a picnic. In the mid- to late 1980s, the calculator business looked a bit like the buggy whip business after Ford mass-produced the automobile. Who needed calculators now that computers—particularly personal ones—were so versatile?

Consequently, there were lots of frustrations within the group regarding the business prospects for calculators. TI was almost in a catch-22 with its calculator business, because it couldn't sell it off, nor did it want to close it down. Most people who knew about the company in 1985 actually thought of it primarily as a manufacturer of calculators. Yet, in reality, that was just "window dressing . . . TI's logo to the world," as Robin recalled. On the other hand, it generated negative profits to such an extent that one Texas A&M alum in the group called it "an Aggie lumberyard, losing money on every log, but expecting to make it up on the volume." In fact, no one really had developed a compelling view of what the opportunity might be, because the dooms-day story was much easier to believe.

Difficult Obstacles Built Common Commitment

Like most doomsday stories, however, this one turned out to be a bit premature. And the first ray of light through the storm clouds was when Tammy Richards led the team in developing a scenario based on both fact and insight, which has stood the test of time. Often Schaar was not the leader of these problem-solving sessions. In fact, this pattern would not be uncommon in most small-group window-jumping sessions in companies where the task at hand is both urgent and difficult. A Tammy Richards and Tom Ferrio, or whoever has the perspective and knowledge required, will rise to the occasion and lead the session—and the team will instinctively support that leadership because it is a thoroughly "natural act." Schaar still recalls the sessions clearly:

> If you go back . . . to window jumping, that's the origin for a lot. . . . [Those sessions] gave everybody really a kind of common view of the world . . . Tammy Richards highlighted . . . that we had a real technology problem by using TI semiconductors . . . we couldn't get as much information to display as our competitors, who were able to use different technology and chip sets.

It made the group realize that it was not only at a critical competitive disadvantage, but also that the only realistic solution was likely to be very unpopular internally, because it would require using non-TI technology. This joint realization—painful as it may have been—was a significant event in the evolution of the window-jumping team.

The Friday afternoon sessions were natural team opportunities, and they were loosely organized and structured. The team discipline came from the group's anxiety and sense of urgency, its complementary skills, and its growing level of common commitment—not from its structure or agenda. Of course, there were scheduled topics to be covered at each meeting, but these didn't comprise the tightly engineered agenda of most formal groups or organization unit teams that run things. The discussions invariably evolved into real problem-solving and action-shaping interactions, where everyone had to roll up their sleeves and do real work together. The work evolved into unpredictable combinations of constructive, as well as confrontational, debates, logical and emotional arguments, fact-based and judgmental decisions, frantic and thoughtful actions—and the meetings often ran into the night. There was little time discipline governing the interaction because they were often in a real team mode!

Certainly the most troubling obstacle they faced was how to break out of the TI technology constraint. The team knew it would have to shape a completely different product road map that was not dependent on TI technology if it was ever to meet marketplace demands. Essentially that meant developing high pixel count displays, which were not possible on TI chips at that time. (Pixel count refers to the number of dots on the display screen, with finer resolutions requiring more dots.) Many of the more attractive margin products required higher pixel counts. Until the group changed its mindset to encompass other chip supply relationships and other display possibilities outside the TI family, it was not about to compete in the high-end markets. As Schaar sums it up, "we simply had to figure out how to do high pixel count products, regardless of the technology required." A number of collective work products grew out of that simple imperative and fueled their growing conviction that TI technology was constraining them in the marketplace. Meanwhile, competitors were gaining significant product advantage in both features and price.

This issue fueled many difficult, extended window-jumping sessions. It also solidified in everyone's mind the need to break free of TI technology. Prior to that time, the essence of the business had been highlighting and selling TI technology. Now it became "what will it take for this to be a viable business," regardless of the technology.

Shifting Roles Becomes a Natural Act

Periodically, Schaar had to step out of his team role to play his formal leadership role of setting targets and making sure budgets were met. In other words, he had no reluctance to apply the single-leader discipline for which executives are paid. As he reflected back on this role, it had a cycle time component to it that is a way of life for most public companies in the high-tech world. When the quarter ends, and stock analysts look at reported results, it is important that the numbers match their expectations. Teams at the top are seldom immune to this pressure—and CEOs or their equivalents instinctively take charge of the process. Teams that run things below the top also feel this pressure and behave in similar ways.

"I think of it as 'dialing for dollars,' " smiled Schaar. "It came at the end of every quarter when earnings were due, and it was up to me to take the number we needed and establish goals for everybody so that it would total up to what was expected of us." Everybody on Schaar's teams recognized what was going on and why it was necessary. Someone had to take charge and make sure the necessary numbers weren't missed, and they all accepted the external influences and tight time constraints that made this executive discipline necessary. This role shift was neither surprising, nor did it inhibit team performance among the subgroups working in other parts of the business, even though some of them would also need to shift out of the team mode to get more timely numbers results.

The Relentless Incremental Climb

The history of TI's successful calculator effort is not one of restructuring jolts, technology breakthroughs, and major change events; rather it was a relentlessly incremental climb in building superior marketing skills and taking over market position one step at a time. In fact, the leadership group, or "core team" as Schaar calls it, has been largely intact for several years, with four of the six having been in place since they launched the effort in late 1984. Since that time, the basic challenge has been sustaining competitive advantage through "ease of use" responsiveness to an extremely diverse and dynamic market rather than operations quality and cost superiority. In fact, virtually all of the product manufacturing has been subcontracted to other companies within a series of relationships, many of which are now over ten years old.

The original leadership group came from one of two skill sets: sharp consumer marketers who learned the technology after joining TI, or sharp engineers who learned marketing on the job. An example of the former is Melissa Stoll, Product Solutions, who came from Beatrice Foods, where she was product manager in the company's imprinted sportswear business. C. B. Wilson is an example of the latter skill set, who honed his operations and engineering skills with TI's consumer computer products group. As Schaar says, "You couldn't really hope to obtain the particular marketing/engineering combination we needed without shaping one or the other skill set on the job." He believes that a disproportionate number of his managers also had MBA degrees of some kind. Although this latter attribute was not an actual requirement, the kind of open, integrative team efforts that characterized the group's management approach lent itself to an MBA mindset.

There was no question that Schaar placed a heavy emphasis on maintaining a diverse set of marketing skills within his leadership group. By contracting out the manufacturing, he has freed his leaders to really concentrate on market analysis, product design, and systems development, thereby creating a competitive advantage in consumer ease of use. Schaar himself had extensive consumer marketing experience in his previous job with Esmark, where he was vice president of marketing for Jensen Car Stereo. He quickly realized that the name of the game in the calculator business had to be superior marketing. There is little question among knowledgeable observers that the group's responsiveness to its target customers has changed the paradigm of the industry (which includes the likes of Sharp, Casio, and Hewlett-Packard) from superior product technology to innovative and responsive marketing capability.

Mixing and Matching to Fit the Need

As I listened to Schaar's description of how the window jumpers worked during their remarkable turnaround success, it was clear that they were often a microcosm of how the better "teams at the top" mix and match both their skills and leadership approaches to obtain team, working group, and individual performance. When pressed to describe the dynamics of the group, Schaar likened it to a set of overlapping circles or ovals that represent different small, interlinked groups—some of which worked as real teams and some, as single-leader units—which grouped and regrouped to allow different skill sets to address different issues and opportunities. As the business gathered momentum, size, and scope, the core group functioned in a team mode less often, although they did break into subteams within the core group, and they often formed subgroups as appropriate outside the core group.

He believes his most challenging task during that period was obtaining resources for his group, and he still finds that he needs to take a strong hand in guiding the group's behaviors to facilitate that end. From the beginning, the group has had to perform within a rather tough set of guidelines or "tight solution space" from top management, which they all describe as follows:

- "Don't ask for money." They had to be self-funding.
- "Don't make waves." Other issues were of higher priority across the corporation.
- "Don't embarrass us." You're in a different game, but our game is dominant.

Their challenge continues to be how to sustain high growth and high return and be self-funding. As they grow in size and complexity, however, it becomes more and more difficult to sustain the kind of team and nonteam balance that was so natural in the window-jumping era. I wanted to learn more about how the group functions today, and Schaar was receptive to my coming back and meeting with the other members of his top team. In the process of making the arrangements for my return visit, however, I learned the hard way how important the factor of time can be in determining the optimum balance between team and nonteam performance for teams that run things at any level.

THE CRITICAL TIME FACTOR

"We've got a minor crisis on our hands," said the anxious voice on my voice mail. It was from my colleague, Tom Hedrick, who had helped me arrange my initial interview with Schaar. "Pallab Chatterjee [to whom Schaar reports] is more than a bit concerned that you are trying to get three days of Richard's team for some damn book effort. He doesn't see what the benefits are for TI. When your assistant tried to line up a three-day block of time, Richard was confused and talked with Pallab about it; understandably, he didn't think it made much sense. You need to give Richard a call!"

At the time, I was in a motel room in Burlington, Vermont. This was all a bit of a surprise to me, but I realized I had been a bit too cavalier in assuming that I could simply delegate the logistics of getting together with Richard's group to my assistant, who wouldn't be able to explain or answer questions that the group would certainly have—including "Why three days?"

The confusion began with an innocent oversight on my part during a breakfast discussion with David Martin, executive vice president of Texas Instruments. Because Martin had been instrumental in arranging for some of my earlier sessions with TI's team at the top, I thought he would be interested to learn of my recent discussions with Schaar. When I told him that I found Schaar's group to be a microcosm of how teams at the top actually struggle to achieve real team levels of performance, Martin expressed mild surprise. Apparently, Schaar's group hadn't scored particularly well in a recent formal assessment process that the company had conducted with several of its leadership teams. As we discussed this anomaly further, it became clear that the assessment may not have taken full account of how teams at the top shift into and out of real team modes. Hence, depending on the mode the group was in at the time of the survey, it might not have been functioning as a team. Martin's interest was piqued, and we agreed that I should see if Schaar might be interested in having us probe further into their situation, with a view to improving leadership team insights for others in the company. When I later reflected with Richard about this team evaluation anomaly, he observed:

> When they did that team evaluation, . . . we needed more teams. . . . So when Dave asked me if I would be interested, and I asked the group if they would be interested, I had a hidden agenda. . . . I knew some of the key areas needed more real team efforts than we had going. . . . [Nonetheless], a number of my

people commented to me after the questionnaire that it could be answered in a number of ways depending on the mode you're in at that point in time, and what you are thinking about.

Sometimes, as Schaar recognized, this reflected a need for more team discipline—but not always. "Not to discount the effectiveness of the team," he observed, "but on the other hand, you do what you have to do to get the job done," and it is not always a team job. Just as with leadership groups at the very top, the tough challenge for any team that runs something is to determine when a team mode is called for and to apply team discipline—without precluding the parallel need for single-leader groups and the executive leadership discipline. Although the two disciplines are seldom natural roommates, they can learn to live together.

Because I was on my way out of town, after my breakfast with Dave Martin, I left an abbreviated message with my assistant to make the arrangements for additional followup interviews with Schaar's group, based on what I thought it might take to meet Martin's interests as well. By the time it got to Richard, the message was a bit garbled. It was no wonder that both Chatterjee and Schaar were concerned.

I called Schaar back to see what I could do to repair the damage. He was understanding, of course, and still willing to proceed if we could help Chatterjee see the value. Schaar suggested that I call Chatterjee, whom, unfortunately, I had never met. Richard also tactfully reminded me that, unlike teams at the very top, he has to shape his top team act within a hierarchical construct that includes a higher-level leader who likes to be involved in unusual events. Teams at the top do not have immediate superiors to worry about like teams that run things down the line.

Chatterjee interrupted my initial attempt to explain with "Look, I just don't understand what's in this for TI that could possibly be worth three days of one of my best leadership group's time. We are in a tough business, and every minute counts for us. Three days is a heck of a lot of valuable time for this team. It would help if you would tell me what we can expect to get out of this"

"Well, I'm not sure I can," I stammered. "Clearly, I will learn a lot about how and why the calculator effort was so successful. . . ."

"But we already know that," Chatterjee interrupted. "What will you learn that we don't already know?"

"Hopefully," I said, groping for reasons, "we will jointly discover ways that Richard's group can more effectively optimize between team and single-leader performance—and also what might work elsewhere in TI."

After a rather long silence, Chatterjee suggested that maybe the three of us should get together for an hour or so and explore whether my preliminary learnings about teams at the top were at all relevant. Based on that, he and Schaar could decide if there was enough value to justify any additional interviews and, if so, which ones. Of course, I agreed to the meeting, but Chatterjee didn't exactly sound particularly eager to hear me expound further on teams—at any level.

I soon discovered, however, that my telephonic impression of Pallab Chatterjee was a far cry from reality. A son of a very well educated family in India, he had graduated from one of India's five IITs (the most demanding academic institutions in that country). He not only earned a coveted gold medal for academic excellence, he was also known as a unique, all-around student because of his activities in both debating and student politics. He came to this country to further his graduate education in electrical engineering at the University of Illinois, where he earned both a master's and a Ph.D. He was the head of research and development at TI corporate before taking charge of the Personal Productivity Products (PPP) business.

His scholastic record attests to his high intelligence and analytical mind, and his progress at TI attests to his people leadership capabilities. Those who work with him find him to be apolitical, with little of the natural arrogance often associated with tough executives. Nonetheless, he is a strong leader with a firm grasp of the executive leadership discipline described earlier. He has high aspirations that are reflected in his performance standards, his managers are judged on their performance results and expected to run their own show, and he holds them accountable for those results as well as for the development of their people.

I learned later, however, that he also has excellent team instincts and clearly recognizes good team performance when he sees it within his organization. He does not, however, believe in teams at any price, particularly when time is a critical element in the performance equation. Early on, it became clear that his telephone bark was worse than his face-to-face bite. He smiled as we introduced ourselves and kept his eyes and ears focused on me throughout our discussion. It was a constructive interchange which ended with his endorsement of my doing a few additional interviews (not three days' worth, however)— provided I would also conduct a session with 25 of his people three weeks later. It was a fair trade.

Moreover, it underlines how very important the factor of time has become in the leadership of high-tech companies. As a result, real teams encounter much more difficulty in applying the discipline that is required for them to realize their potential. Although this is true at any level, as the calculator group illustrates, it is most severe at the very top. Chatterjee's concern over three days of time for one of his better-performing leadership groups is not only understandable, it is compelling.

THE IMPACT OF SIZE AND COMPLEXITY

My next session with the rest of the window jumpers was most revealing. To begin with, their recollections of the window-jumping era confirmed most of what I had learned from Schaar. More importantly, however, they drew a number of intriguing contrasts with the early days and described how their situation changed as the business grew in size, scope, and complexity. That picture was beginning to sound surprisingly parallel to the dilemmas and challenges that teams at the top face.

The most obvious change has been in the size of the core group. The original 5 has now grown to 17, and they are seldom able to convene as a group. When they do, individual agendas and preset time constraints determine the interactions. It is seldom that the entire group even comes close to functioning in a real team mode. Even the core team doesn't often function in a team mode nowadays. At the last meeting of the total leadership group several months ago, two new opportunities for subteams were identified (one for new markets and one for new applications). One group hasn't even had time for an organizational meeting, and the other has yet to do any substantive work together.

The problem is not in the lack of collective task opportunity: both are of vital strategic importance to the company, and both have a number of collective work product needs. Certainly, the time constraints on both are a factor, but thus far there has been little effort even for single-leader working groups. The problem, as described by the group, appears to lie in the composition of the expanded membership and the prevailing attitudes. The newer members of the group haven't experienced the "trial by fire" that produced such strong commitment among the window jumpers. Therefore, they are more easily swayed by day-to-day issues and quarterly expectations. Strategic issues with longer time frames and increasing complexity are much easier to delay.

Some opportunities, however, are pursued with natural work groups, involving a "subset" of the core team members, along with some of their reports. Some approach real team performance. An example is a subset of the calculator group, which faces the challenge of developing products to penetrate the learning business, where a number of important collective decisions needed to be made—and were—about specific product offerings. There are also subsets of core members working on reengineering the product development process. These natural subsets occur most often with the original team members, because they have a history of working together and enjoy the interaction and relationships. Also, as Robin points out, their individual work locations are near one another, thereby making it much easier to collaborate. Finally, their working experience together in the past enables them to use technology as a strong surrogate when face-to-face work is difficult.

In the last couple of years, information technology has given them much more capacity and flexibility for these subgrouping efforts. Lotus Notes, in particular, facilitates their doing real work together and creating important collective work products without always having to come together physically. As with any innovation, one fears the tendency to overuse it and not get the effectiveness into a collective work product that would come from being in the same workplace. So far, however, the group views it as an underutilized tool that can truly help real team efforts.

Nonetheless, most problems tend to be dealt with by a strong individual, coupled with organizational unit groups of direct reports rather than real teams. For example, when product problems occur, the head of quality or production will act as the leader of a group to solve the problem; strong sales managers work with front-line sales teams on problems in the same way. Time pressures and complexity force the use of single-leader working groups over teams in many situations that all would acknowledge as potential team opportunities.

Over time, Schaar aspires to migrate back to more and more real team efforts, but he is the first to admit that things are not yet in balance. Although he is quick to acknowledge the need for single-leader working groups, he really wants to obtain more real team performance. The tradeoffs in getting the right balance in his leadership group are no different than those for leadership groups at the top of large corporations. Team performance suffers as the leadership group increases in size, as the time constraints become more severe, and as the required interactions become more complex.

The core group believes that working groups have become more common than real teams. The main reason is that potential team members seldom have the luxury of time to work together on generating solutions. It has become too difficult to take time from their more pressing individual leadership tasks and still achieve their individual performance goals. Some members come to the leadership group discussions with closed minds; they won't even consider alternative end products and solutions. That attitude has the effect of closing out other potential team members with different perspectives and skills (prompting Tammy Richards to say at one meeting, "Don't use my hands if you don't want my head"). There is an obvious opportunity for the leaders to take actions that might propel the working groups toward more team solutions (conflict integration, enforcement of team discipline, clarification of collective work products), which Schaar clearly recognizes. In fact, that is one of the primary reasons why he increasingly encourages more open discussions of this situation.

Whatever the issue, opportunity, or problem, however, both the composition of the subgroup and the mode within which it operates must fit the collective work needs. Because of the strong team capability of the window jumpers, they can still ensure that real team discipline is sustained when the situation calls for it. Their history has given them an advantage in this regard, because they had to learn the team discipline at the same time they were developing their individual executive leadership discipline. Growing up with the two disciplines working together has given them the inherent advantage of being able to identify potential team opportunities. It also helps them guard against the problem of such opportunities' being overlooked or overridden by a more ingrained executive leadership discipline. The challenge they face, however, is exactly the same challenge faced by teams at the top of much larger and more complex institutions.

RULES OF THE GAME FOR ALL LEVELS

This example highlights most of the elements of team performance at the top, as well as for teams that run things at other levels. It also illustrates the rules of the game that apply to any leadership group—top, middle, or front line—that wants to find its hidden potential for team performance.

1. ***Pick your team shots wisely.*** A team mode is not the only mode for leadership groups seeking higher performance. You cannot expect to function as a team all the time. Team efforts work only in situations where collective products and multiple leadership contributions offer high value. Some of these may be recurring, as was Schaar's window-jumping act; some may be one time, as was Mobil's top organization redesign. C. B. Wilson at TI observes that the window jumpers may be falling into the trap of picking too many "hollow team opportunities." This not only distracts the core team from the real issues that warrant their time, but also builds skepticism among others about the value of real team efforts. The best leadership groups learn to avoid those situations and focus on spotting the real team opportunities in advance, rather than waiting to be jolted into a team mode by the "big event." And those leadership groups that attempt to address all performance challenges as a single team invariably become frustrated, if not jaded.

2. ***Consider each of your options carefully.*** Single-leader working groups, enabling teams, organizational unit teams, and total enterprise teams all have their place and role in a high-performing organization. The best leadership groups at any level make use of all the options they have. They are not wedded to one approach, and they make a concerted effort to learn and modify several

approaches. Both Schaar and Chatterjee are continually on the alert for different ways to shape leadership approaches to attain higher levels of performance. Although they are understandably protective of their time and people, they are also determined to consider any and all options that offer performance potential. Although they may sometimes be "out of balance," they are never satisfied to remain so.

3. ***Make the critical tradeoffs consciously.*** Single-leader working groups are fast, efficient, and powerful when the leader really does know best. "Enabling teams" are best when the real work actually will be done by individuals working their piece of the performance puzzle largely on their own. Real teams require time to form and shape a working approach, but once in the team mode, they will achieve much higher performance results in any situation requiring collective work products. Schaar recognized this when he encouraged his group to submit to Dave Martin's formal team evaluations. He also recognized that the team mode made little sense during "dialing for dollars." The tradeoffs that matter most are speed versus collective work values, clear leadership direction versus shared leadership capacity, and skill versus representational needs. To a lesser degree, the team skill of the available group leaders is a factor to be considered.

4. ***Apply the discipline that fits.*** It is usually more natural to apply the executive leadership discipline the higher up in the organization you are—simply because that is how large organizations are expected to work. As a result, teams at the very top overuse that discipline to the detriment of team performance. This can also be true for leadership groups down the line, but increasingly the reverse is true. While Schaar's group initially relied very heavily on real teams, they are becoming increasingly sensitive to letting other disciplines thrive as well. The right balance, however, is a moving target that is never easy to hit. Once they experience the power of team discipline, it is just as easy for top groups to overuse it as it is for them to overrely on the executive leadership discipline.

5. ***Learn different leadership roles.*** Beware of your "personal favorite" leadership approach or role. For example, most people who have attempted to be team leaders in a situation that demanded

strong leadership direction will remember the frustration and confusion that resulted. The reverse is also true, although at top levels it is much easier to overlook the missed team performance potential. But the leadership roles go well beyond these two. Chatterjee plays a strong team sponsor role within his executive leadership discipline. Schaar works in different roles to guide both team and single-leader efforts. Going forward, however, he recognizes the opportunity to capitalize even more on his role in several areas. These include picking the right skill sets for teams, instilling more discipline on long-term versus short-term team and working group efforts, integrating conflict when members try to force compromise solutions, and legitimizing the team efforts by taking a more active role. Those who are wedded to "what has worked in the past for me" will always suffer the loss of important leadership capacity within themselves as well as others. Schaar's attitude is anything but that.

6. *Set aside open-ended times for working together.* Regardless of the mode or level in the organization, it is important for "teams that run things" to set aside time to do real work together. The tighter the agenda and schedule, the less likely real work can occur. Schaar's window-jumping sessions are a good example of an open agenda, and he is already moving to use more of that in recent meetings of his enlarged leadership group. Certainly there is always a need for meetings that are tightly structured; it is an efficient way to accomplish many aspects of what leadership groups must do. For that reason, it is often a good idea to consider different kinds of meetings—some tightly structured and some open-ended. The latter will often produce "team mode" behaviors, even if they are short-lived. As these modes occur and are recognized, it behooves the group to consider how to take better advantage of the performance capacity they represent.

CONCLUSION: SHARING MUCH COMMON GROUND

Despite obvious differences, teams at the very top share much in common with top teams down the line. Certainly, teams that run things down the line have the advantage of being closer to both the marketplace and the workplace. They are also less encumbered by broad corporate leadership issues and demands. Members are also more likely to have had recent, hands-on experience with teams that perform and are therefore less disposed to follow executive leadership discipline no matter what. Conversely, leadership groups at the very top have the advantage of greater authority to shape initiatives, obtain resources, and establish priorities. They can choose to work in many different modes and membership configurations without seeking the approval of those above (although the board certainly defines their solution space).

Regardless of level or position in the organization, however, teams that run things can discover significant performance potential by paying attention to the following fundamentals for team performance at the top:

- Executive leadership discipline can be integrated with team discipline; the two are not mutually exclusive, but the right balance varies over time.

- Any leadership group can function in a team mode if it learns to be realistic about identifying real team opportunities and rigorous about applying the discipline required for real team levels of performance.

- No leadership group can function in a team mode all the time because each member must discharge important individual leadership and performance responsibilities as well.

- Mastering the ability to shift modes and membership configurations is the key to tapping the potential for teams that run things at any level.

- Changing roles is more important for the leader than changing styles; however, not every executive can lead a real team.

- Identifying significant collective work products, and matching skills to those products, usually requires looking beyond the "direct reports," as well as avoiding the imperative of "all the direct reports."

- When in a real team mode, the leadership must shift to fit the task at hand to capitalize on the full leadership capacity of the group.

- Every leadership group should be able to identify the most important (six to ten) team opportunities within its jurisdiction; it is a useful "team function" for the group to formally identify such opportunities at least once a year.

- Leaders need to provide forums to create common understanding of the group's history, business drivers, and overall business circumstances; without that understanding, it is hard to share performance commitment.

Most importantly, however, do not leave team performance to instinct and chance. If you simply rely on the big, unexpected events to jar your group into a team mode, you will leave a great deal of performance potential untapped. Figure 8.1 is a simple decision tree that lays out the critical decisions, options, and considerations that are important for any leadership group that wishes to obtain a better balance of team and nonteam performance.

Figure 8.1
OPTIONS FOR "TEAMS THAT RUN THINGS"

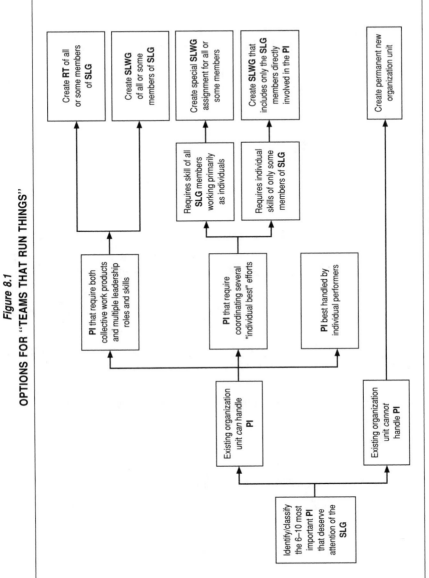

Note: **PI** = Performance Issues; **SLG** = Senior Leadership Group; **RT** = Real Team; and **SLWG** = Single-leader Working Group

Discipline, Alignment, and Balance

T HIS BOOK STARTS by asserting that a different mindset is needed for thinking about teams at the top. It argues that a team at the top cannot be a team all the time. It suggests that "less is better than more" *undisciplined* team efforts at the top, because that can lead to real team performance where it counts. It also maintains that different issues, problems, and opportunities at the top require different modes of behavior among the senior leadership group. And "all the direct reports" should not be trying to become a team.

Three simple ideas or themes are central to this argument. Because they are at the heart of increasing the leadership capacity and performance capability of the team at the top, this final chapter expands on those themes:

1. **Discipline.** Integrating real team and executive leadership disciplines to energize, rather than stifle, initiative and performance.

2. **Alignment.** Applying more than one kind of mechanism to align the behaviors and decisions of people throughout the organization.

3. **Balance.** Blending the primary elements of organization and the flexible units into a balanced leadership approach which optimizes leadership capacity and performance.

In each case, the notion of "either/or" must give way to an attitude of using the best of both (or several) approaches to increasing leadership capacity at the top over time.

DISCIPLINE—AN ARTISTIC ANALOGY

Discipline is at the heart of high performance, be it for an individual, a team, or an entire institution. It was defined earlier as *a set of rules or training that corrects, molds, or perfects*. We have already explored in detail the importance of learning to integrate the discipline required for team performance with the discipline required for individual executive performance. Both disciplines are essential for obtaining world-class performance in any organization. Rather than belabor that point, let me turn to an analogy from the art world: the New York City Ballet Company (NYCB), unquestionably a world-class performer in its field. Its relentless integration of disciplines (dance, music, leadership, and team) has been noteworthy in its ability to energize rather than stifle innovation and creative excellence.

One of the great cultural achievements of our time, the New York City Ballet has delighted audiences around the world with its near-flawless performances for over 50 years. Created by the vision, artistic talent, and relentless pursuit of perfection of George Balanchine and Lincoln Kirstein, the company is without peer in the world of creative and classical dance. In a truly unique leadership effort, these two men built an institution that has successfully survived both of them and is to this day devoid of "stars" but overflowing with talent. Many artistic organizations have tried in vain to duplicate both the results and the approach that reflect the genius of Kirstein and Balanchine. The NYCB history speaks for itself:

> The New York City Ballet, one of the foremost dance companies of the world, *is an organization unique in the artistic history of the United States* [emphasis added]. It alone, of all our institutions in the performing arts, trains its own artists, creates its own works, and performs in its own home.[1]

The Starting Point

The success of this nonpareil institution, however, is not as much a team story as it is a story of vision and discipline. Kirstein's vision was an American ballet company, rather than a group of imported artists performing for American audiences. Hence, the starting point must be a school where native (American) dancers could be trained and disciplined in the art of dance by the greatest ballet masters he could obtain. When he encountered George Balanchine in London in 1933, he realized he had found a kindred spirit with the ballet mastery he had envisioned.

I first met Kirstein over lunch at a small restaurant in New York City shortly before I was to join the board of directors for the School of American Ballet (the unique school that preceded and continues to develop the talent for the company). At that meeting, he emphasized the importance of having the same kind of discipline in the overall governance of the school and the company as he and Ballanchine insisted on in the artistic performance of the company. In fact, it was primarily because of their unflagging devotion to their art form and adherence to disciplined recruiting, training, and practice that enabled the school to survive and the company to flourish.

Few business challenges require the discipline that world-class ballet performances demand, with the years of special study, endless practice, and tireless dedication to excellence, if not perfection. Dancers, carefully selected for their artistic and physical potential, learn the basics of the ballet as individuals in a highly disciplined program. Yet they also apply those basics within very disciplined team configurations. Choreographers work as creative individuals but also team with dancers and composers to achieve a superior performance. The New York City Ballet Company exists because its leaders created a special environment wherein team performance is prevalent, but never dominant. More than anything, the NYCB is a study of the disciplined pursuit of perfection, which balances and integrates leadership, organization, talent, and art in a context that delivers world-class performances over time. It all reflects a unique set of beliefs and core values.

A Unique Set of Beliefs

Obviously, the NYCB is vastly different in size, purpose, and composition from the corporate organizations and senior leadership groups that are the focus of this book. Nonetheless, its integration of disciplines and its balanced leadership approach provide a useful analogy. First and foremost, the NYCB organization reflects a powerful core ideology first engendered by Kirstein and Balanchine. Their vision of what it could become, the artistic values to which they adhered, and their personal commitment to make it happen are found in only a very few organizations that achieve excellence and deliver value over time. The company has never wavered from a set of basic beliefs which persists today:

- Focus on the dance as a primary and independent art form, not merely a secondary accompanying one.

- Obtain and develop the best American talent when it is young enough to shape and inspire.

- Screen for unique artistic sense as well as physical attributes, and develop each dancer to the fullest extent of his or her potential.

- Maintain an environment of excellent performance, not dependent on "stars," wherein the achievement is measured, as Balanchine maintained, "through the eye of the audience."

Holding to these beliefs, Kirstein and Balanchine utilized diverse processes, structures, and programs, as well as teams and nonteams, to approach perfection. It was an aspiration they could not hope to attain, but never ceased to approach. Although the two men seldom functioned as a real team because their individual contributions came in separate areas, they fostered the team efforts of others in selecting and creating scores, recruiting talent, training performers, and developing innovative programs that mastered everything from popular jazz to classical symphony. Within it all, they never lost the power of the individual performer, which is at the heart of their art form. At the same time, their rejection of the "star system" that characterizes most ballet companies enabled them to obtain unique team efforts both on and off stage. It is unlikely, however, that they needed to concern themselves with untapped team potential, for their focus on the performance challenge led to both disciplined team and nonteam efforts when needed.

So is it really fair to suggest that "teams that run things" in any business situation need to worry about their untapped team potential? Can't they simply let the performance challenges pull team behaviors forth at random? Unfortunately, very few business enterprises have the core ideology, performance ethic, and clarity of purpose that allows the NYCB the luxury of obtaining teams at random. Nor are most companies as disciplined in their application of these standards. Obviously, building a world-class ballet company is not the same thing as running Microsoft, Compaq, Enron, Morgan Bank, or IBM. Those organizations are changing almost daily as they strive to create faster, bigger, and more diverse enterprises, so maybe they need to pay *more* attention to unleashing their potential for more team performance at the top. The truth is, you need *not* consider how to tap into team potential at the top unless and until:

- You truly believe that real teams can outperform nonteams in situations with high upside performance potential.
- You are convinced you are not getting real team efforts when and where you need them most.
- You respect and need the flexibility value that teams add to the stability and consistency of formal structure and process.
- You are willing to devote the time, effort, and hard work required to *integrate the disciplines* required for real team levels of performance with those required for superior individual executive performance.

Otherwise you might as well continue to rely on the executive leadership discipline that favors individual performers and single-leader working groups—which has been good enough to guide large, stable, and established institutions for years.

It stands to reason, however, that senior leadership groups in almost any complex business setting that do not avail themselves of team performance are losing valuable leadership capacity as well as performance capability. Moreover, the discipline required for real team efforts is most often missing at the top. That is why this book focuses on the hidden potential for teams in the top leadership group's portfolio of leadership approaches and alignment mechanisms.

ALIGNMENT—MORE THAN ONE WAY

Alignment is what organization theory is mostly about: getting the decisions and actions of people aligned to achieve a performance result that is more than what could be accomplished otherwise. The decisions and behaviors of people in a large organization can be influenced by many different things, not all of which are under the control of the top leadership group. Some of the more important determinants of people's behaviors, in fact, come from within the individuals themselves, from their personal beliefs and intrinsic character traits.

Over time, of course, leaders can change the composition of their workforce by replacing the people whose attitudes and skills don't fit with the needs of the enterprise. Getting the right people in the right places is certainly as important as getting real teams in the right places; but, it is only one step along the long, winding path to aligning the behaviors, decisions, and performance of large numbers of people.

Pall Corporation, in Chapter 5, is a good illustration of a company that has shifted its alignment emphasis from informal teams to process. The current leadership now concentrates more on its core process and matrix structure to produce the alignment it needs for performance across the company. Its departure from the more informal team efforts of its founders reflects the increased size, scope, and complexity of the company. It also reflects a different leadership philosophy at the top. In recent years, a new leadership group has adopted a formal matrix structure which allows rapid communication across products and geographies to resolve technical and customer issues. While the top leadership group meets several times a year in standing committees (such as Operating and New Directions committees) to exchange information and resolve conflicts, these committees also identify and approve high-potential opportunities for middle-management teams, such as new product development and geographic expansion. These teams supplement the overall formal process and matrix structure. Top management believes that their process includes and fosters easy communication both up and down the chain of command and between functions, to resolve customer service, product development, and quality issues.

For example, Arnold Weiner (Industrial Processes) meets on an ad hoc basis with the COO, Derek Williams, and other senior vice presidents to discuss specific product requirements or distribution issues. Their processes and close relationships, based on many years of working together, allow the leaders to reach decisions within one or two meetings—hence, they believe that extended so-called team efforts are both impractical and unnecessary.

In other words, there is more than one way to achieve alignment, and it is important to consider the appropriate balance for any institution in light of its marketplace and workplace situation—and given its fundamental aspirations, values, and beliefs.

A Common Base of Beliefs

The better leaders tackle the challenge of alignment by getting their leadership group to buy into a basic vision of the enterprise, supported by clear values and business strategies. *Built to Last*,[2] by James Collins and Jerry Porras, provides convincing evidence that truly visionary companies (those that have led their industries for many decades) draw great alignment strength from a set of values or "core ideology" that seldom changes over time. But, however a company's vision and values are shaped to begin with, they need to be periodically reinforced among the top executives as well as throughout the organization. When these reinforcing efforts work, they result in a senior group that shares a common understanding and commitment to a basic foundation on which performance alignment depends. And alignment is the name of the implementation game in any dynamic organization: *leaders must somehow align the decisions and behaviors of managers and workers to deliver value to customers faster and better than the competition.*

The Primary Elements of Alignment

Leaders have four primary elements or mechanisms to help them align the decisions and actions of their people. Two of these—formal structure and management processes—are relatively stable or given in the near team. The other two—forums (small groups) and networks—are much more flexible. All four, however, must be applied in ways that are consistent with the basic beliefs and aspirations just described. Figure 9.1 spells out the specific tools that make up each of these elements:

1. *Formal structures.* Most people look to structure—the organization's formal "boxes and lines"—as the primary map for aligning behaviors. It is usually the first place leaders turn when they want

to realign or change behaviors—"Let's reorganize (again!). Let's redefine what people are supposed to do, and change the reporting relationships." Changing the design of the formal structure always gets people's attention, but it seldom produces a lasting change in behaviors without the help of some "matching set" of formal processes and informal networks. For that reason, I consider the formal structure of an enterprise as analogous to the scaffolding in the construction of a building. It provides necessary support for much of the work that must take place in the beginning, but as the building takes shape and can support itself, the scaffolding becomes less critical.

Unlike a building's scaffolding, however, the formal structure in an organization seldom becomes completely unnecessary. People always need to know what they are responsible for and to whom they are responsible—even when those touchstones vary with the dynamics of the marketplace. The structure usually remains a primary alignment element because it helps to ensure order and consistency over time. It provides stability and essential advancement tracks for individuals. Who's in charge here? and How do I get ahead in this place? are not trivial questions, even

Figure 9.1
THE PRIMARY ELEMENTS OF ALIGNMENT

Formal structures	Management processes	Informal networks
Functional departments	Business	Communication
Product/market divisions	Management	Best practice
Geographic sectors	Communication	Market/customer
Line of business	Education and training	Intelligence
Business unit		Distribution
Matrix		

Permanent forums
• Councils
• Committees
• Work groups

Ad hoc forums
• Informal work groups
• Temporary teams
• Task forces

within paradigms of organizational thinking that would have us eliminate the hierarchy.

There are many different kinds of formal structures that can work effectively, as Figure 9.1 suggests. In fact, you can find successful enterprises that rely heavily on each of those listed, just as you can find successful enterprises that have put together a mosaic of different kinds of structures. Although the formal structure is an important element in the alignment of decisions and behaviors—and although different structures fit different strategies and business situations—you cannot rely on structure alone for superior execution. A lean and flat organization structure may be clear and efficient, but it is not necessarily flexible or responsive.

Thus a formal organization structure provides essential support for much of the work of any enterprise, particularly in the beginning. But, as the other elements of organizational alignment take shape and can support themselves, the formal structure carries less of the alignment load.

2. ***Management processes.*** *Process* is a word that is applied in many different, often-confusing ways today. Simply defined, it is a prescribed set of work or action flows that deliver value to customers. Usually these action flows cut across the formal hierarchy, and thus can be thought of as "horizontal" relative to the more "vertical" formal structure. Proponents of process management argue that a well-designed process can eliminate much of the unnecessary up-and-down approval requirements in a vertical structure and thereby facilitate information, work, and product flows to and from the customer. Both real teams and single-leader working groups are often essential parts of most well-designed processes. The emphasis on horizontal flows and core process focus has been on the increase recently. A number of good companies are relying on strategically designed processes to advantage.

Many enterprises like Pall Corporation believe that well-designed processes at the top create alignment that is different from, and complementary to, hierarchical structures. Seldom, however, can process alignment alone provide the same flexibility and responsiveness to deal with unexpected changes in the marketplace that the more versatile team approach can provide. Hence, it makes sense to use teams in conjunction with both process and structure—not to view one approach as a replacement for the other. Those who rely primarily on process disciplines are as likely to miss significant performance opportunities as those who overrely on structure. *High performance is a game of disciplined alignment—not one of processes versus teams.*

3. **Forums and small groups.** A forum is any small group of people (council, committee, work group, or team) that meets regularly to enable people to communicate, interact, and work effectively within and across both formal structures and processes. Mobil's recent reorganization (Chapter 5) provides a good example of the diverse forums required in any effective organization. Starting at the top, its senior leadership group, called the Executive Office, often functions as a real team as well as a single-leader group, depending on the issue or subject at hand. Two other senior groups, the Executive Development Council and the Opportunity Development Council, often functioned in a team mode, particularly when they were shaping the new processes designed to accelerate leadership development. They recently formalized a forum of the dozen or so leaders of the operating businesses (which had been meeting as an ad hoc group) to supplement these processes. As these new forums and processes took shape, however, each of the councils could function more efficiently in single-leader working group modes.

The role of the senior leadership group in any organization is to ensure whatever forums (teams or nonteams) are required to link actions across and within the formal structures and processes. Sometimes that role may warrant some or all of the group to function in a real team mode. More often, however, their role is to establish other forums and small groups, and to ensure that the appropriate disciplines are applied.

4. **Informal Networks.** Perhaps the most neglected element or aspect of organizational performance—at least in a design sense—are the informal networks. Virtually no organization can function well without some set of informal networks. They allow people to connect with one another outside the formal structures, processes, and forums. They also help meet important social needs of people in the organization. And, as Tom Timmins of Mobil reminded us in *Real*

Change Leaders, "if you restructure first, you destroy the informal networks"[3] that made the old structure work. As a result, any new organization structure will likely work at less than full effectiveness until such networks can be re-formed.

Unfortunately, senior leadership groups seldom worry about the informal networks when they are reorganizing—largely because they assume that networks will develop as they are needed, more or less automatically. Over time this may be true, but in the short term, or in a critical change situation, a network deficiency can be a problem that should not be ignored. Certainly, in any broad-based action program, the necessary communications will take place only if the social networks pick up on them. Since both teams and single-leader working groups can be quick, effective ways to correct network deficiencies, it is worthwhile for senior leaders to periodically identify critical informal network problems that might be addressed by a leadership team or by another team that it might sponsor. This is particularly true whenever a different formal structure or management process is being launched or redesigned.

Each of these primary elements offers different advantages and disadvantages for aligning people's actions. It is the integrated combination of all four, however, that represents the best potential alignment solution for any complex organization. The basic challenge senior leadership groups face in achieving their aspirations and strategies for the corporation is in the integration of these elements. This is also where the flexible units come into play and can make a big difference. The "flexible units"—teams, working groups, and individual performers—often constitute the best options that a senior leadership group has to accomplish cross-structural and process integration. They are extremely useful in merging complementary actions both within and across the stable elements of alignment.

Much of this is obvious to executives who already know about structure, process, networks, and forums because they encounter them daily. However, if you ask your favorite executives to name the most important things they employ to align the decisions and behaviors of their people, you are likely to get a wide variety of inconsistent answers, such as clear roles and responsibilities, stretch goal setting, individual accountability measures, compensation incentive plans, training programs, policy guidelines, procedural rules, and various ways to punish the wayward behaviors. Some executives, of course, will cite versions of one or more of the primary elements of alignment—but seldom in terms that recognize the varying advantages and power of each, and even more rarely in terms that suggest conscious integration.

Despite the fact that these basics are very well known, too few executives understand their relative importance, why they are the primary alignment mechanisms, or how best to *optimize performance by relying on all four—rather than overrelying on one or two of them.* More importantly, perhaps, there is a widespread tendency at the top to overlook the special power and complementary advantages of the flexible units. Senior leadership groups are in the best position to utilize the flexible units in a balanced context, because they control— and can therefore modify, redesign, or reinforce—most aspects of the formal structure, process, forums, and networks.

BALANCE—BLENDING IT ALL TOGETHER

My discussions with several of the top executives referred to in this book are captured in the conceptual picture (Figure 9.2). This integrating framework is intended to illustrate how both the primary elements and the flexible units come together in a balanced leadership approach. To that end, the chart positions the various design elements that can help align decisions throughout the organization. Starting at the bottom of the chart, the key elements are illustrated as follows:

1. ***The base of aspirations, values, and core beliefs.*** These provide the fundamental foundation and focal point for the performance of any specific institution or enterprise. They provide both the directional imperatives and the "rules of the game" that differentiate one institution from another. In high-performing institutions, they seldom change over time.

2. ***The primary elements of alignment.*** These are the formal structures and management processes, as well as some of the informal networks and forums. All can serve to help leaders align the behaviors and decisions of people at various levels, including the top.

They can and should change as performance opportunities and issues require.

3. **The top triangle of "flexible units."** This includes individuals, single-leader working groups, and real teams. They operate within any and all configurations of the other elements. The triangle also includes the senior leadership group or groups—which may function in any or all of the three flexible unit modes.

4. **The formal and informal "constructs."** These are more encompassing notions that refer to what most people think of as the formal organization and the informal organization. Together, they encompass all of the other elements on the chart, and are described in detail on pages 702 to 707 in Chapter 4. Their position on the chart is to indicate that the left-hand side includes elements that tend to favor the formal organization, whereas the right-hand side

Figure 9.2
THE BALANCED LEADERSHIP

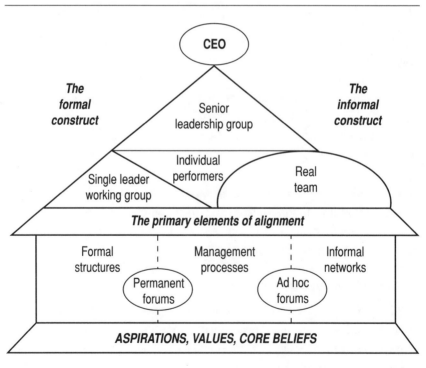

includes elements that tend to favor the informal organization. Obviously, teams and working groups can be effective on both sides.

The CEO, of course, presides at the top. The fundamental point of the chart, however, is that the top leadership challenge is to utilize and integrate within the formal and informal construct—using all of the elements of alignment with both discipline and wisdom to optimize the leadership capacity of the total organization. Unfortunately, this is easier said than done.

Using "Flexible Units" to Optimize Performance

The more interesting elements for teams at the top appear in the upper and right-hand portions of Figure 9.2 , which depict the "flexible units" and informal networks that are increasingly essential to both high performance and culture change. Although these include real teams, they also include single-leader working groups and individual performers. The senior leadership group can avail itself of these various "flexible units" either instinctively or consciously both within and outside of its own ranks. Enlightened leaders like some of those discussed earlier (Noto, Olson, Platt, Reed, and Shapiro) may have instinct on their side, but I believe they are also well advised to address these options explicitly and consciously.

The left side of the chart (single-leader units and formal structures and processes) is what the former culture at many established giants like Mobil and Citicorp relied on most heavily for aligning the decisions and behavior of people throughout the organization. *This "left-side bias" is typical of most large, mature, successful companies.* The challenge facing a senior leadership group is to develop its capacity to bring the right side of the chart into much sharper focus throughout the company. In Lou Noto's mind at Mobil, for example, this implies that his senior leadership group must become increasingly adept at mastering three emerging, but difficult, senior leadership group skills:

1. The ability to differentiate individual, team, and nonteam opportunities.

2. The flexibility to shift into and out of the team mode as different situations require.

3. The confidence and trust to shift the leadership role among the members.

The company's overall leadership capacity will also depend on its ability to help change leaders across the broad middle of the organization to develop this same leadership insight, flexibility, and capability. At the same time, Noto's Executive Office members remain adamant about the need to continue to utilize single-leader units and individual performers in concert with real teams—not an easy balance to maintain.

The Value of "Real Work"

There is little question that both individual and collective efforts deserve top executive attention. There is also little question of the tendency for most top leadership groups to leave too little time for the substantive work that can lead to real team levels of performance. Unfortunately, most senior leadership groups do not provide time for the real work that team performance demands. Abraham Zaleznik published an insightful article on real work for both managers and executives in the *Harvard Business Review* in 1989. Zaleznik, a distinguished professor of organizational behavior at Harvard, argued that too many in the management ranks of large corporations tend to rise above both the workplace and the marketplace. As a result, they are not engaged in much real work—which he defined as that which is directly concerned with making the product and delivering value to the customer. He also observed that the higher one is in the organizational hierarchy, the greater the tendency to oversee, delegate, and critique—rather than to problem-solve, design, and create. Without a significant component of "real work" on the agenda of a top leadership group, there is but limited chance of team performance within or among the group.[4]

Although this is more of a problem at the very top, it is not a trivial issue for leadership groups down the line. Many leadership groups do not consciously set aside the time required for substantive work like that we saw in the "window-jumping" sessions at Texas Instruments. Without the time for substantive work together, team performance is impossible at any level.

CONCLUSION: A MIX OF OPTIONS— NOT A "TEAM AT THE TOP"

Expanding and tapping into the leadership capacity throughout the organization is important for virtually any enterprise that anticipates growth and change, be it Mobil, Enron, Champion, or Ben & Jerry's. It doesn't seem to matter whether the company is large or small, industrial or financial, global or regional—leadership capacity appears to be in short supply at all levels.

Perhaps this has always been true and will always be true—we can never have enough leadership capacity. On the other hand, just because the aspiration is elusive does not mean that we can afford to ignore the need. Within the context of leading a complex enterprise to an increasingly high set of balanced aspirations, team performance is but one of several approaches that must be considered. At the same time, I believe it is the *one with the most potential for immediate results—as well as the one that is most neglected within top leadership groups.*

The forces at work in any large organization can easily result in groups at the top that have no interest in learning how to increase their team performance. Paradoxically, these very same leaders are often in serious pursuit of more leadership capacity. Yet they continue to overlook the value of the team approach in optimizing the leadership capacity of any small group. Real teams know how to shape working approaches that exploit the leadership capabilities of all their members. They also know how to develop those individual and collective capabilities to the fullest.

What worries me most when able leaders are first exposed to these notions of shifting modes and membership configurations at the top is their tendency to conclude, "We already do that." Discussions of these options among senior leadership groups invariably produce a great deal of head nodding, knowing glances, and side comments of support—followed by sighs of relief because "we don't really have to worry about being a team after all—we just have to keep delegating work to subgroups." An understandable reaction, as I have argued that much of what the best leaders do instinctively is what works best for teams at the top. I have also indicated that most personal styles do not need to change, that executives should not feel guilty about functioning as single-leader working groups, that subgroups are usually the best way to obtain team performance, and that strong individual leadership counts for a lot. Moreover, it is clear that unexpected major events will probably trigger team behavior anyway. "So don't we already do it that way?" is a common reaction. Besides, most executives are more comfortable being the head buffalo. As Ron Burns might say, "If you want to be the head buffalo, you have to be prepared to lead the herd pretty much on your own."

So why not just keep doing it the way you are most comfortable? The answer, of course, is because *instinctive adherence to executive leadership disciplines will snuff out team discipline.* Any senior leadership group may get team performance in the truly crucial situations, but it will not get it in many other important opportunities. Understanding the difference between team and nonteam situations is not enough. Learning how to recognize those differences, consciously making the tradeoffs between speed and performance, integrating the two disciplines, and applying the right discipline at the right time is more than instinctive to most leaders who run things at any level.

The good news is that team performance at the top is much more doable than commonly assumed. The bad news is that most small groups that "run things" can only obtain it by changing their approach, learning new skills, applying multiple disciplines, *and* doing more real work together. For that reason, this book concludes by offering the reader a Diagnostic Guide (Appendix C) for CEOs and other top leaders who truly want to obtain greater leadership capacity and team performance capability within their senior leadership groups. The guide is a set of simple questions which, if answered honestly, can help pinpoint where a senior group may have significant upside potential relative to its collective leadership approach by obtaining a better balance in its use of teams and nonteams.

Integrating real team performance with executive leadership performance requires both a sharp understanding of the difference between the two disciplines required and a relentless determination to integrate the two. It is hard work, counterintuitive, and outside the comfort zone of most senior executives. Nonetheless, it is well worth the effort.

A Glossary of Team Terms

Action flow: A set of actions (involving several people) intended to create a sequential, coordinated result.

Collective skills: The skills of more than one person applied together to achieve a unified or integrated result.

Collective work product: The tangible result of several members of a group applying different skills to produce a performance improvement not achievable by any one member alone.

Consequence management: A philosophy of managing that rewards and punishes people based on an individual's results or the consequences of each person's actions.

Core ideology: A set of basic beliefs, values, and aspirations.

Direct reports: Those who report on a direct line to a single leader; the immediate subordinates of the leader.

Enabling team: A single-leader working group or organizational unit that interacts to encourage and motivate one another to higher levels of individual performance.

Executive discipline: A set of implicit rules that executives follow to enforce individual accountability and consequence management; synonymous with *single-leader discipline.*

Formal construct: The formal organization; namely, the specific roles, responsibilities, and lines of communication that determine who reports to and informs whom.

High-performance team: A real team whose levels of commitment to its purpose and goals exceed those of all other like groups and whose members are also committed to one another as individuals. This unit is rare, and its members remain committed to one another well beyond any formal team experience.

Informal construct: The informal organization; namely, the relationships, informal networks, and communications that exist or take place outside of the formal organization.

Informal networks: The connections between people as individuals or within ad hoc groups that cut across and around formal structures and processes.

Leadership capacity: The amount of leadership talent and time within any group of people, organization, or institution.

Mode of behavior: How people in a group work together, as a team, as a working group, or as a nonteam.

Mutual accountability: More than one person accountable for the results.

Nonteam: Any group interaction or behavior that does not fit the definition of real team; it may or may not achieve a collective purpose.

Organizational unit team: The permanent group of direct reports in any unit, program, task force, function, or process. *The group is defined by the organizational structure;* it may or may not function as a single-leader unit or working group, enabling team, or real team.

People systems: The process, networks, programs, incentives, and work rules that determine human behavior in an institution.

Performance issue: A specific problem or opportunity, the resolution of which will influence the performance of the enterprise or organization.

Performance unit: A group of people and resources that offers the potential for collective performance results.

Potential team: A work group that has yet to discipline itself relative to the five "team basics" that determine real team levels of performance.

Power alley: The specific positions or individuals who have the most influence on decisions and rewards throughout a vertical segment of the organization; synonymous with *political system.*

Process: A set of work and action flows that determine individual and group behaviors.

Pseudoteam: A working group that does not recognize any performance purpose to its interactions.

Real change leaders: Resourceful midlevel leaders who know how to bring out the resourcefulness in others in change situations.

Real team: A small number of people with complementary skills who are committed to a common purpose, performance goals, and approach for which they hold themselves mutually accountable.

Single-leader working group: A group of people assigned to a leader who determines their work tasks and sets their performance objectives. The leader also integrates or combines their results and holds each person accountable for his or her individual contribution.

Team at the top: The senior leadership group of an institution or organization; synonymous with *all of the leader's direct reports.*

Team basics: The five elements required for real team levels of performance: size, purpose and goals, skills, working approach, and mutual accountability.

Top team: A group of executives who may function as a real team or as a single-leader working group.

Total enterprise team: All members of an enterprise, business unit, or large functional department who develop a high level of commitment to the purpose of the enterprise and whose personal support for one another is beyond that of normal organizational relationships.

Working approach: How a small group works together to apply its multiple-person skills to products or problems of the group.

Working group: Any small group of people who come together to accomplish a common purpose or set of results; synonymous with *work group.*

Working vision: A simple phrase—closer to 5 words than to 50—that helps a group see clearly where they are headed and why it matters; it grows out of the work they do together.

Work skill: What an individual has learned to do that has direct or indirect value in an organization.

Team Discipline Reprise

T HROUGHOUT THE BOOK, I refer to the basic elements of team performance. Many readers will recognize these elements from *Wisdom of Teams*, but I would like to summarize them here. However, nothing in this material is intended to do other than emphasize the importance of these elements in achieving team levels of performance, particularly at the top. A real team is a powerful and flexible performance unit, but it is not a complex unit. Too often, well-intentioned leaders fail to achieve the potential of team performance simply because they do not adhere to these basics. The elements derive from the definition of a real team, which I believe to be no more complicated than this working definition from *Wisdom:*

> a small number of people with complementary skills who are committed to a common purpose, performance goals, and approach for which they hold themselves mutually accountable.[1]

A brief summary of the elements spelled out by this definition is a useful reference:

1. *A small number.* Because they must work together on collective work products, it is difficult for more than 20 or 30 people at any level to really function as a team. The optimal size to ensure team levels of performance seems to be fewer than 10; larger groupings can succeed, but often they are better advised to function in subunits.

2. *Complementary skills.* The key to the extra level of performance results that real teams achieve derives from the mix of skills that multiple people possess that cannot be obtained in one individual.

There are three categories of skills, all of which need to be in balance relative to the team's purpose and goals: technical or functional expertise, problem-solving and decision-making capability, and interpersonal skills.

3. ***Common purpose and performance goals.*** A common level of commitment to a meaningful purpose and set of goals is absolutely essential to motivate and energize a team. Without this clear direction and means of tracking progress, the momentum and collective energy required for extra levels of team performance do not occur.

4. ***Commitment to a common working approach.*** Every team must evolve a way of working together that capitalizes on the unique skills that each member represents. This approach not only must take account of the skill mix, it must also take account of members' availability and special constraints. Otherwise, the collective work products that constitute the extra performance specifics cannot be produced.

5. ***Mutual accountability.*** A group cannot function as a real team until it is able to hold itself accountable for the achievement of its purpose and performance goals. This mutual accountability is best expressed as "we hold ourselves accountable" as opposed to "our superior or leader holds us accountable."

These elements are just as mandatory in teams at the top as they are at any other level. Unless this discipline is rigorously applied in any would-be team situation, the extra levels of performance that real teams achieve are unlikely. All elements must be adhered to rigorously—there is no margin for error.

Applying that discipline at the top is just as important as it is elsewhere in the organization, but it appears more difficult for three reasons:

■ The commonly accepted "discipline" of executive leadership is often in conflict with one or more of the basic elements of team discipline.

■ The time available for potential teams to achieve real team levels of performance is more compressed.

■ Risks of team mistakes and failures can be much higher and more costly.

Diagnostic Guide: *Obtaining Team Performance When It Counts*

THIS GUIDE HAS BEEN DEVELOPED for CEOs and other top leaders who seek to improve the leadership capacity and performance capability of their senior leadership groups. Each category contains a set of questions, which, if answered negatively, are cause for concern. The subquestions also point to the action required for a better balance.

1. **Mindset.** Does your group maintain an open, neutral mindset with respect to its mode of behavior?

   –Can it differentiate the many performance issues and situations— those that require real team behaviors from those that don't?

   –Are the members comfortable working with both team and non-team efforts?

   –Do they really know (from personal experience) that both teams and nonteams add value at the top?

   –Do they also know when to "feel guilty" about perpetuating a single-leader unit where a team makes more sense—and vice versa?

2. **Leadership capability.** Does your group have the collective capability to apply more than one leadership approach?

–Can most of the members avoid being addicted to—and actually work outside of—their "personal favorite" modes of leadership behavior?

–Have most members had recent firsthand experiences with real team behaviors and results?

–How many members can actually function as real team leaders as well as working group (nonteam) leaders? Can most of them play "subordinate" team member roles when appropriate?

–Can several shift their role and style in leading a small group?

3. **Performance ethic.** Are the performance results of the group (as a group) more important to the members than the group's composition, mode of behavior, or individual roles?

–Do legitimate team purposes and goals regularly take priority over individual achievements and rewards?

–Are subgroup efforts common within the "team at the top," and do such groups hold themselves mutually accountable for the group's collective results?

–Do you add ad hoc members with relevant skills to address critical issues and opportunities? Do they function the same as regular members?

–Do you exclude regular members when a real team issue doesn't require their skills or experience?

–Do the members believe it is more important to have all of the members involved than it is to obtain real team levels of performance?

4. **Meetings and work sessions.** Does your group shape and vary its working approach to tap the leadership capacity of all the members?

–Does the group establish different kinds of meetings and work sessions to accomplish different purposes and goals?

–Does the time, format, and setting vary to fit the work agenda?

–Does the composition of the group usually fit the skill and work requirements of the agenda?

–Can the group function as a team even when its members are not all physically in the same place?

5. **Key litmus tests.** Does the group recognize the importance of collective work, multiple and shifting leadership roles, and mutual accountability in determining what discipline to apply?

   –Does the group make a conscious effort to shape collective work products in ways that encourage team performance?

   –Are you and other members comfortable shifting the active leadership role to fit the leadership needs of different situations?

   –Do group members consciously find ways to hold themselves mutually as well as individually accountable for all legitimate team efforts?

   –Does the group consciously apply the above tests to performance issues and challenges before, during, and after the fact?

6. **Leadership capacity and balance.** Does the senior leadership group avail itself of all its options for obtaining alignment and performance throughout the organization?

   –Does it avoid overreliance on the formal structure and management processes?

   –Does it design and shape informal networks as well as use them?

   –Does it assess its performance as a group as well as assess the performance of individuals and the company as a whole?

Notes

Introduction

1. From *"The Spirit of Haida Gwaii,"* a pamphlet published by the Canadian Embassy in Washington, D.C., which describes the sculpture and the artist.
2. Jon R. Katzenbach and Douglas K. Smith, *The Wisdom of Teams* (Boston: Harvard Business School Press, 1993).
3. James C. Collins and Jerry I. Porras, *Built to Last: Successful Habits of Visionary Companies* (New York: Harper Business, 1994), 41.
4. "Conflict and Strategic Choice: How Top Management Teams Disagree," *California Management Review* 39, no. 2 (Winter 1997): 43.
5. Donald C. Hambrick, "Fragmentation and the other problems CEOs have with their top teams," *California Management Review* (Spring 1995).
6. Sydney Finkelstein and Donald C. Hambrick, *Strategic Leadership: Top Executives and Their Effects on Organizations* (Minneapolis: West Publishing Company, 1996).

Chapter One

1. Quotations without sources throughout book are from personal interviews with the author.
2. Jon R. Katzenbach and the RCL Team, *Real Change Leaders: How You Can Create Growth and High Performance at Your Company* (New York: Times Business, Random House, 1995), 228.
3. Ibid., 229–230.
4. Richard J. Hackman, *Groups That Work (and Those That Don't)* (San Francisco: Jossey-Bass, 1990), 84.
5. Jon R. Katzenbach and Douglas K. Smith, *The Wisdom of Teams* (Boston: Harvard Business School Press, 1993).

Chapter Two

1. Jon R. Katzenbach and Douglas K. Smith, *The Wisdom of Teams* (Boston: Harvard Business School Press, 1993).
2. Richard J. Hackman, *Groups That Work (and Those That Don't)* (San Francisco: Jossey-Bass, 1990).
3. Douglas C. Hambrick, "Fragmentation and other problems CEOs have with their top teams," *California Management Review* (Spring 1995).
4. Ibid.
5. Katzenbach and Smith, *The Wisdom of Teams.*

Chapter Three

1. Robert P. Bauman, Peter Jackson, and Joanne T. Lawrence, *From Promise to Performance* (Boston: Harvard Business School Press, 1997), 2.
2. Ibid., 35.
3. Ibid., 71.
4. Ibid., 91.
5. Ibid., 88.
6. Jon R. Katzenbach and the RCL Team, *Real Change Leaders: How You Can Create Growth and High Performance at Your Company* (New York: Times Business, Random House, 1995).
7. James C. Collins and Jerry I. Porras, *Built to Last (Successful Habits of Visionary Companies)* (New York: Harper Business, 1994), 43.
8. Ibid., 45.

Chapter Four

1. James A. Belasco and Ralph C. Stayer, *Flight of the Buffalo* (New York: Warner Books, 1993).
2. Jon R. Katzenbach and Douglas K. Smith, *The Wisdom of Teams* (Boston: Harvard Business School Press, 1993).
3. Pauline Graham, ed., *Mary Parker Follett—Prophet of Management, A Celebration of Writings from the 1920s* (Boston: Harvard Business School Press, 1995), 90.
4. Henry C. Metcalf and L. Urwick, eds., *Dynamic Administration: The Collected Papers of Mary Parker Follett* (London: Pitman, 1941), 30, also referenced in Graham, *Mary Parker Follett,* 90.
5. Graham, *Mary Parker Follett,* 90
6. Ibid., 191.

Chapter Five

1. Robert P. Bauman, Peter Jackson, and Joanne T. Lawrence, *From Promise to Performance, A Journey of Transformation at SmithKline Beecham* (Boston: Harvard Business School Press, 1997), 35.
2. Ibid., 35.
3. Ibid., 93.
4. Ibid., 100.
5. Ibid., 158.
6. Ibid., 160.
7. Ibid., 170.
8. Jon R. Katzenbach and the RCL Team, *Real Change Leaders* (New York: Times Business, 1995).
9. Ibid.
10. Donald K. Clifford, Jr., and Richard E. Cavanagh, *The Winning Performance* (New York: Bantam Books, 1985).
11. PR Newswire, 1990.

Chapter Six

1. Deborah G. Ancoma and David A. Nadler, "Top Hats and Executive Tales: Designing the Senior Team," *Sloan Management Review* (Fall 1989).
2. Fred "Chico" Lager, *Ben & Jerry's, The Inside Scoop: How Two Real Guys Built a Business with Social Conscience and a Sense of Humor* (New York: Crown Publishers, 1994).
3. Ibid., 148–150.
4. Ibid.
5. Richard J. Hackman, *Groups That Work (and Those That Don't)* (San Francisco: Jossey-Bass, 1990), 84.

Chapter Seven

1. Daniel Goleman, *Emotional Intelligence* (New York: Bantam Books, 1995), 34.
2. Pauline Graham, ed., *Mary Parker Follett—Prophet of Management, A Celebration of Writings from the 1920s* (Boston: Harvard Business School Press, 1995), 69.

Chapter Nine

1. "NYCB Company History," www.nycballet.com/NYCBHist.html.
2. James C. Collins and Jerry I. Porras, *Built to Last: Successful Habits of Visionary Companies* (New York: Harper Business, 1994).

3. Jon R. Katzenbach and the RCL Team, *Real Change Leaders: How You Can Create Growth and High Performance at Your Company* (New York: Times Business, 1995), 212.

4. Abraham Zaleznik, "Real Work," *Harvard Business Review* (January–February 1989).

Appendix B

1. Jon R. Katzenbach and Douglas K. Smith, *The Wisdom of Teams: Creating the High-Performance Organization* (Boston: Harvard Business School Press, 1993), 45.

Index

About the Author

Jon R. Katzenbach is a director of McKinsey & Company, Inc., where he has served the senior executives of leading companies for over thirty years. His experience includes work with both public and private sector clients from the industrial, financial, and consumer industries. He has also served a variety of nonprofit institutions. He specializes in issues involving corporate governance, organization, and leadership.

He is the author and coauthor of numerous publications and books, including *The Wisdom of Teams: Creating the High Performance Organization*, and *Real Change Leaders: How You Can Create Growth and High Performance at Your Company*.